ROLLING VOICE

INTERNATIONAL COLOURING BOOK OF

Swear Words

AND FUNNY CUSSES

ADULT COLOURING BOOKS

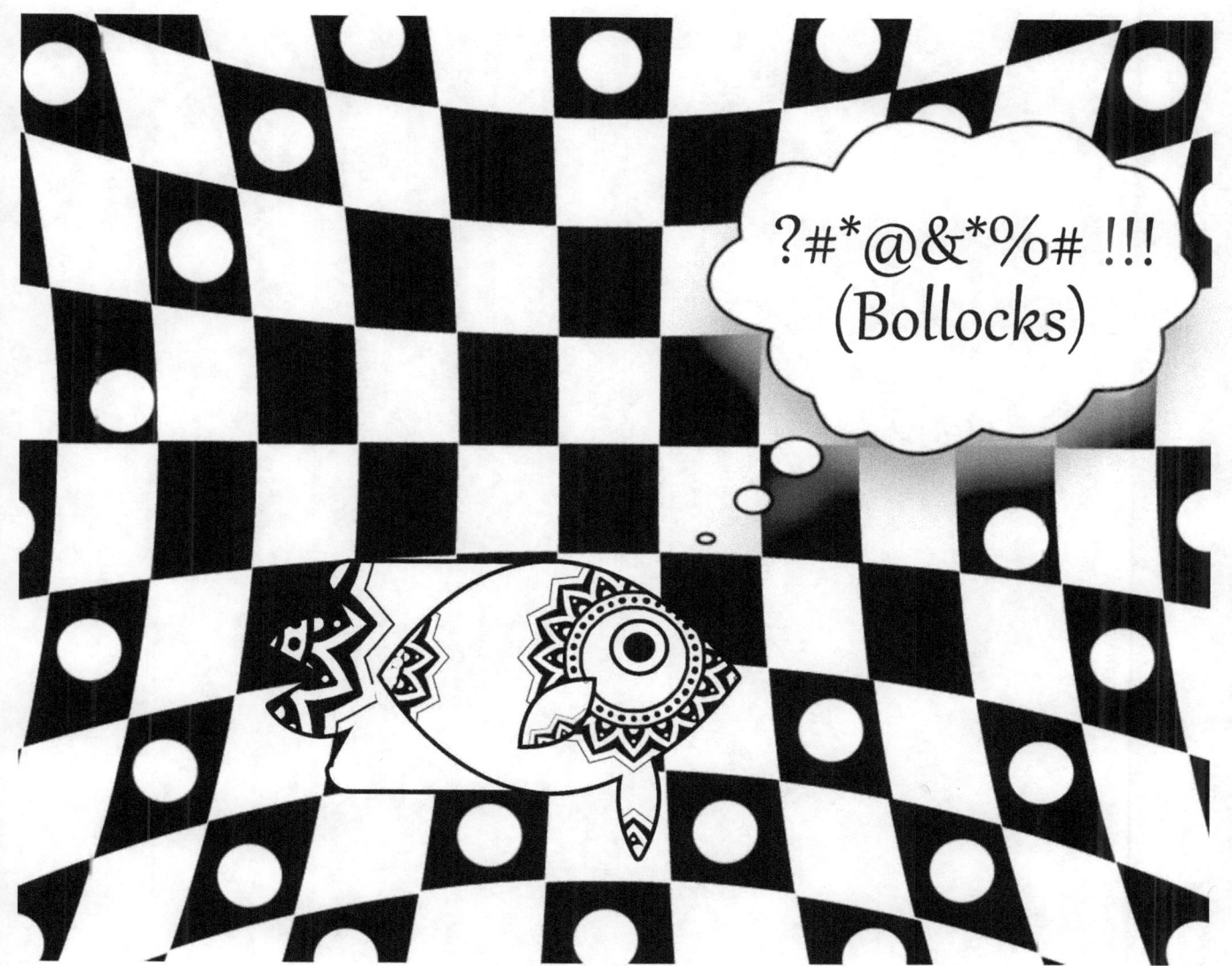

Printed in the United States of America

First Printing, 2016

ISBN-13 : 978-1530376667
ISBN-10 : 1530376661

Rolling Voice Publishing
33 Lower Park, Chartfield Avenue
London, SW15 6QY
United Kingdom

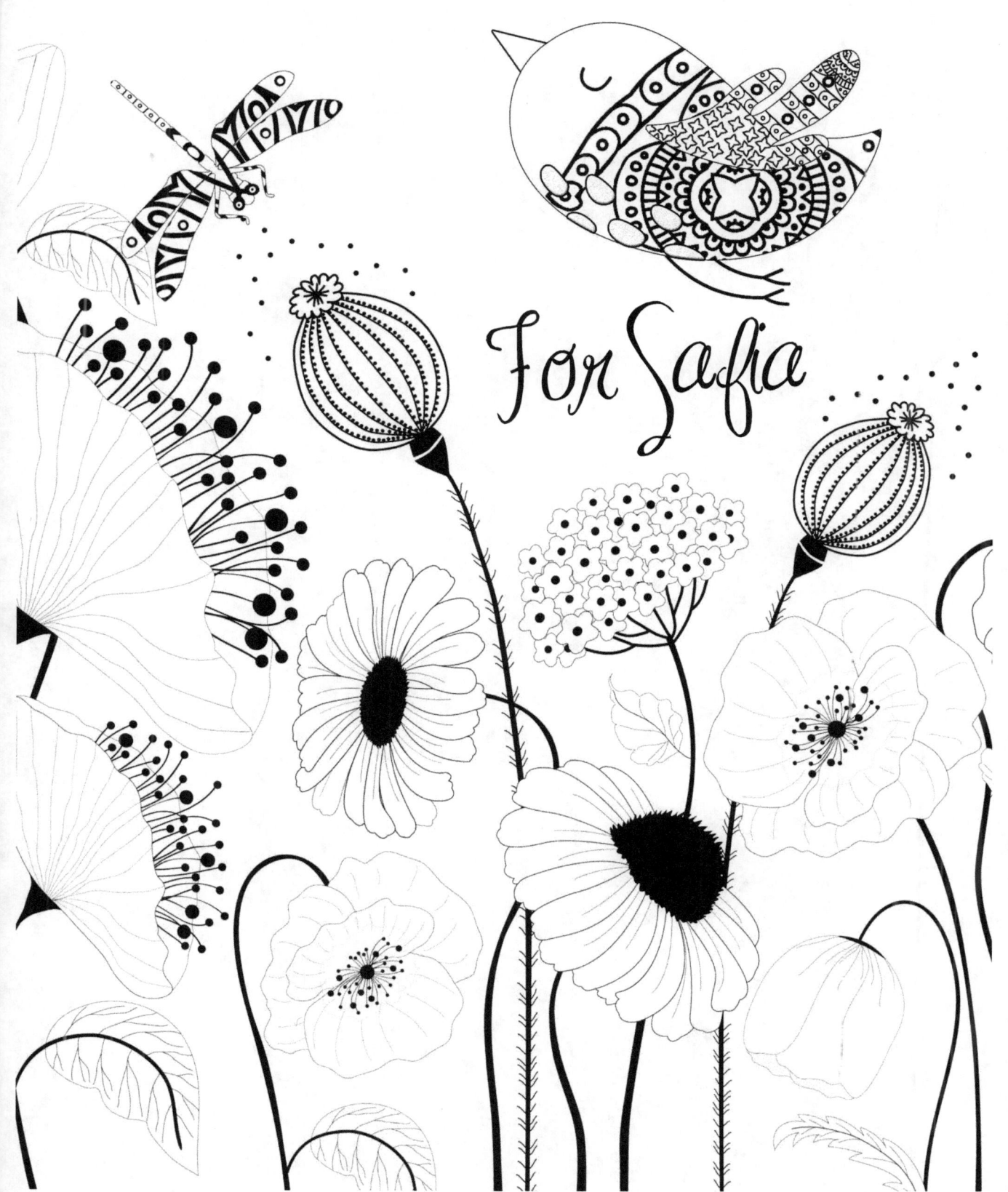

For Safia

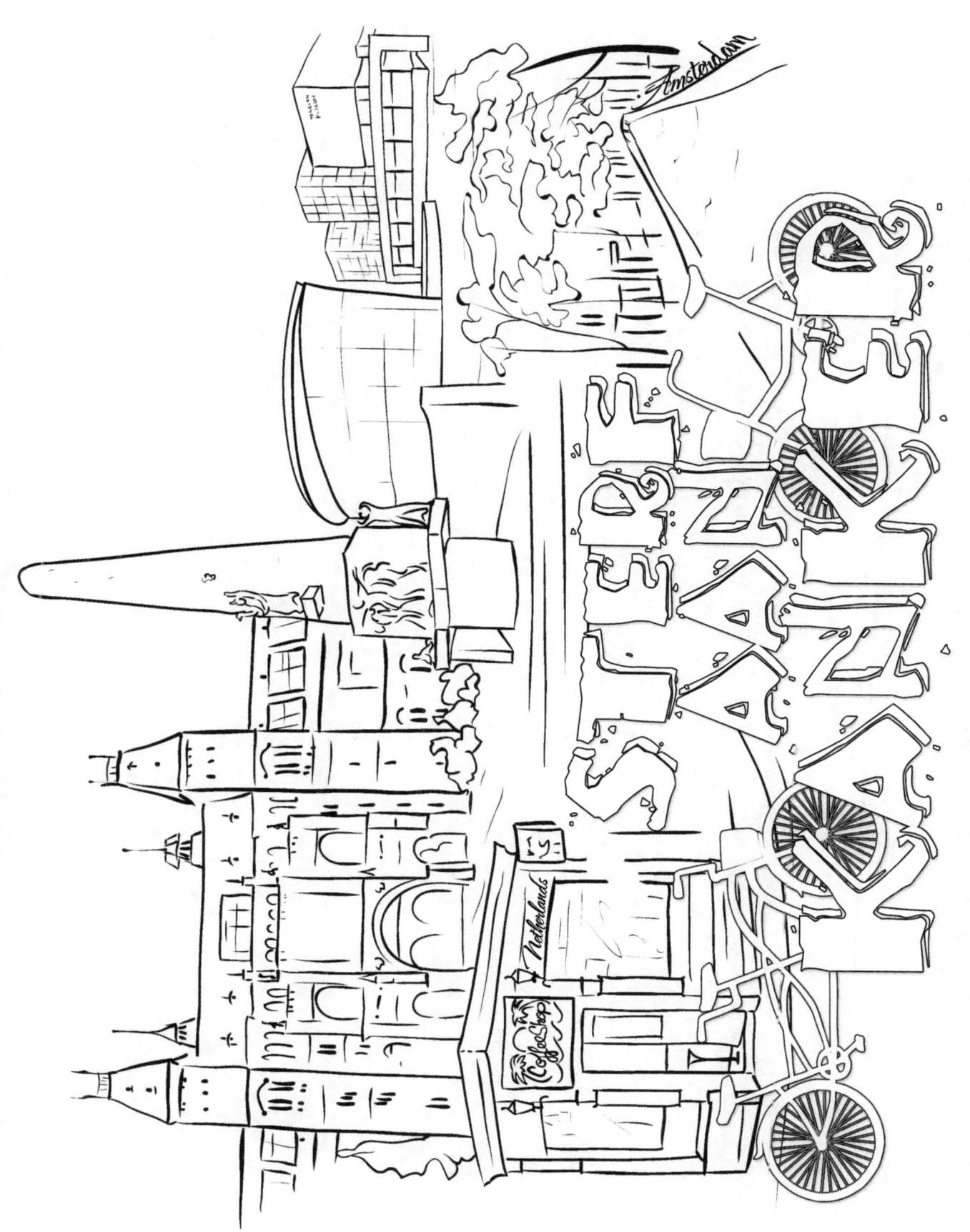

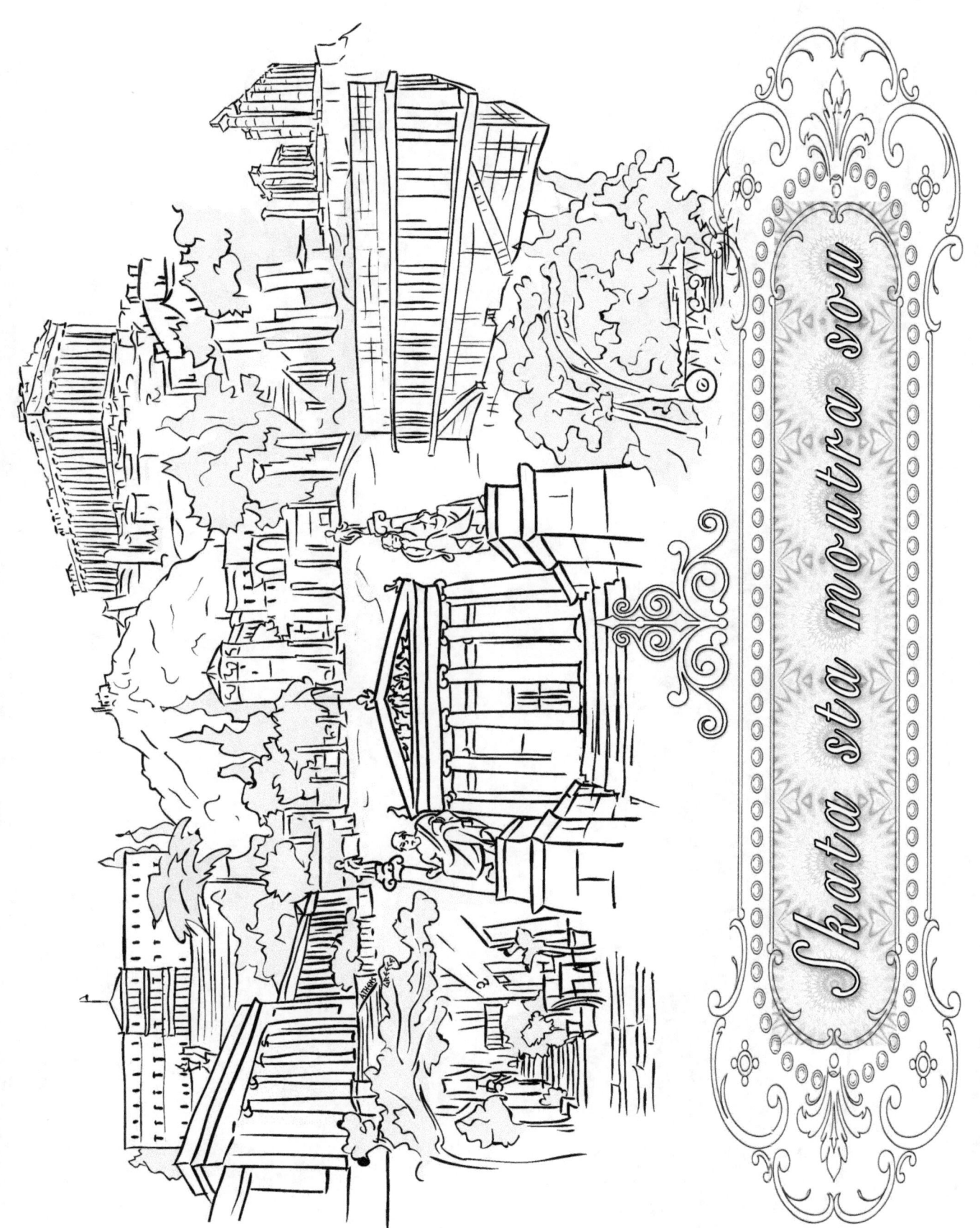

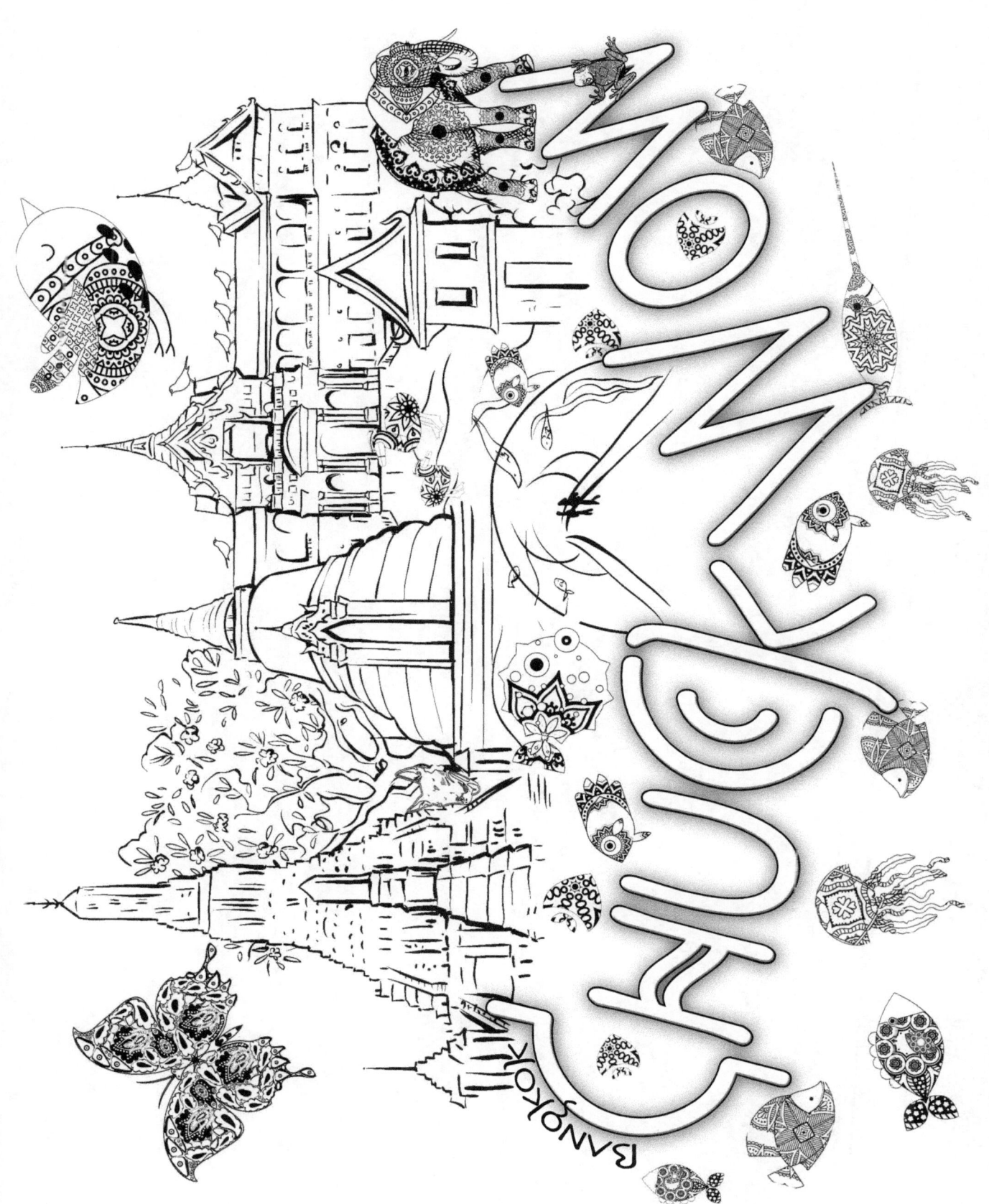

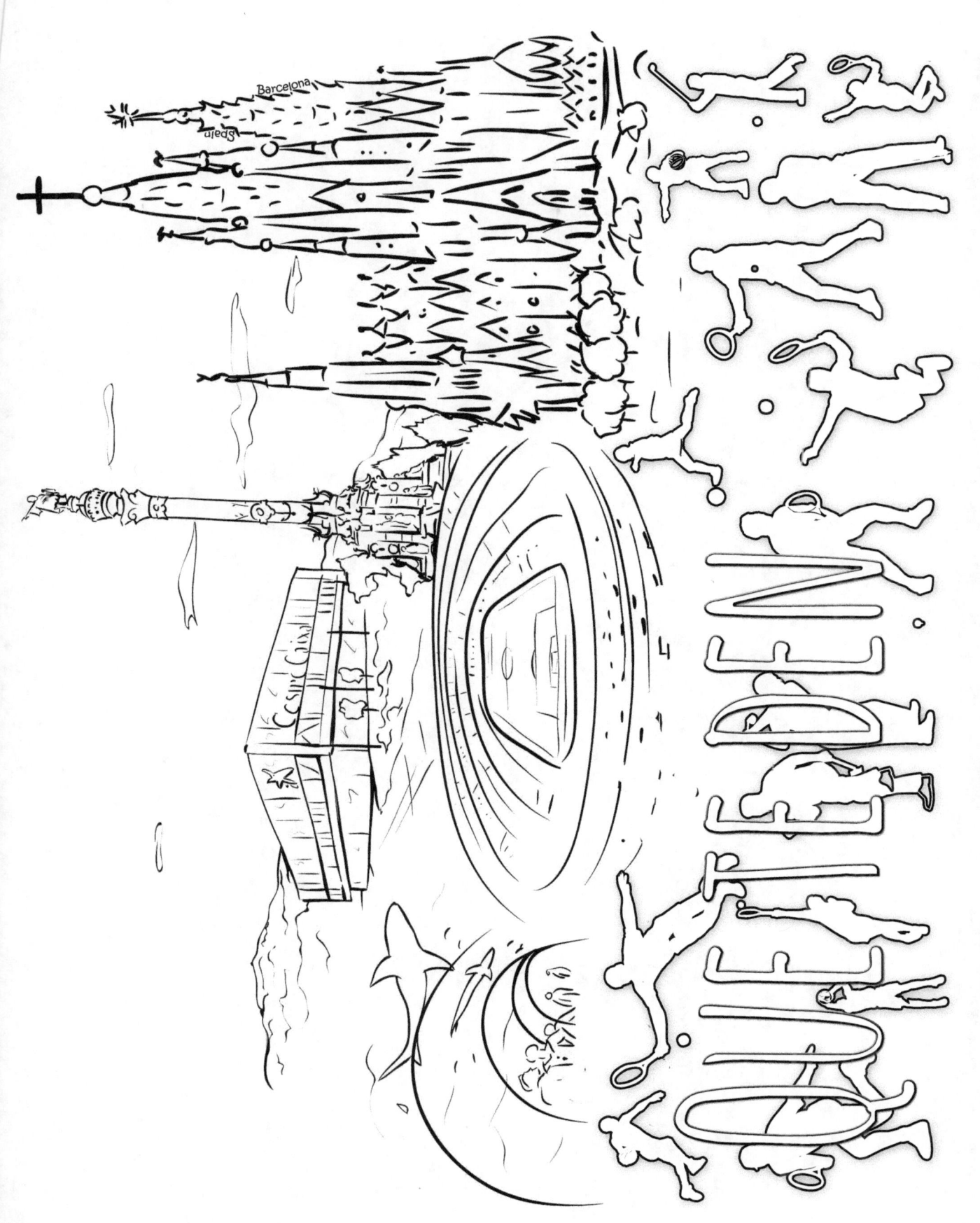

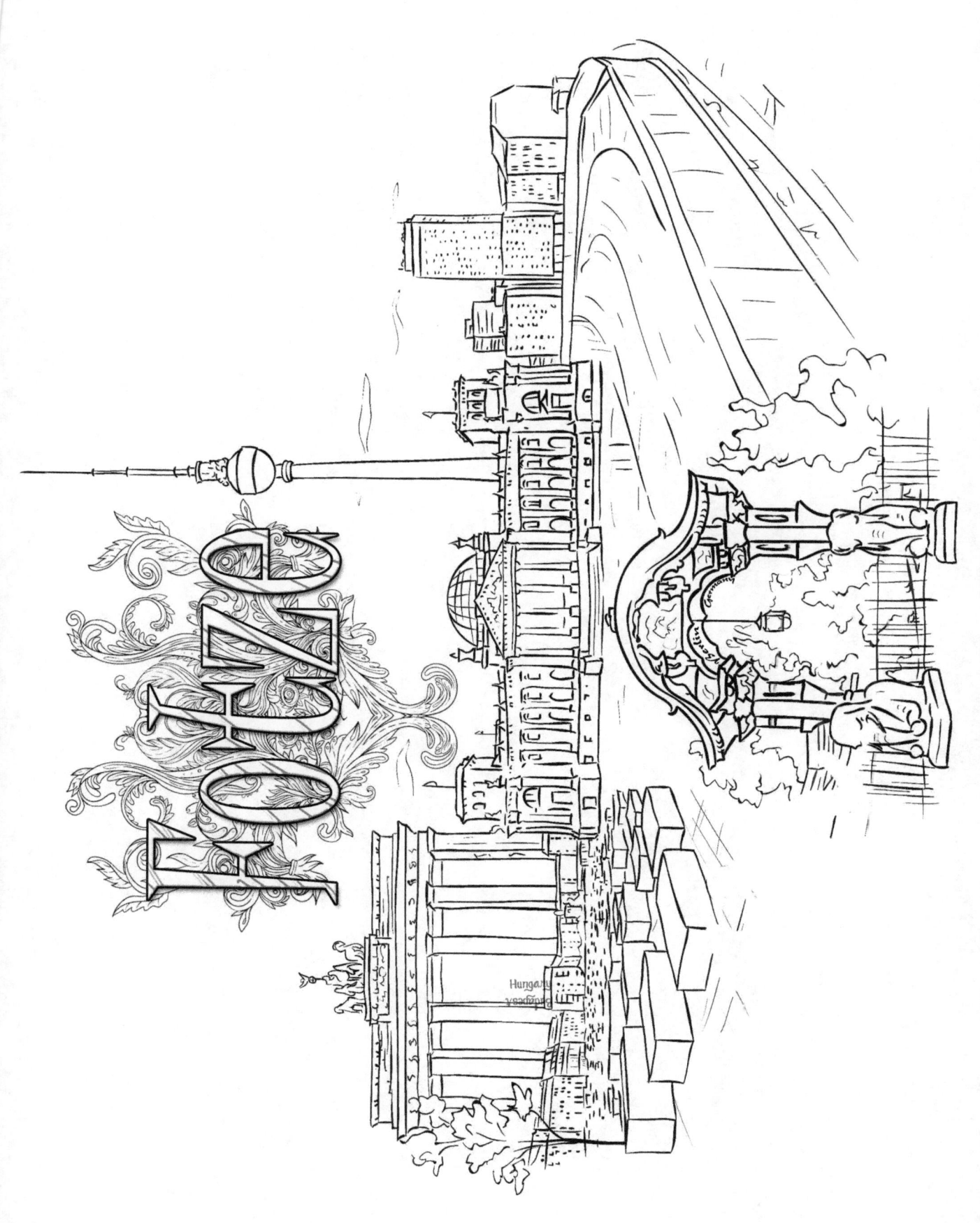

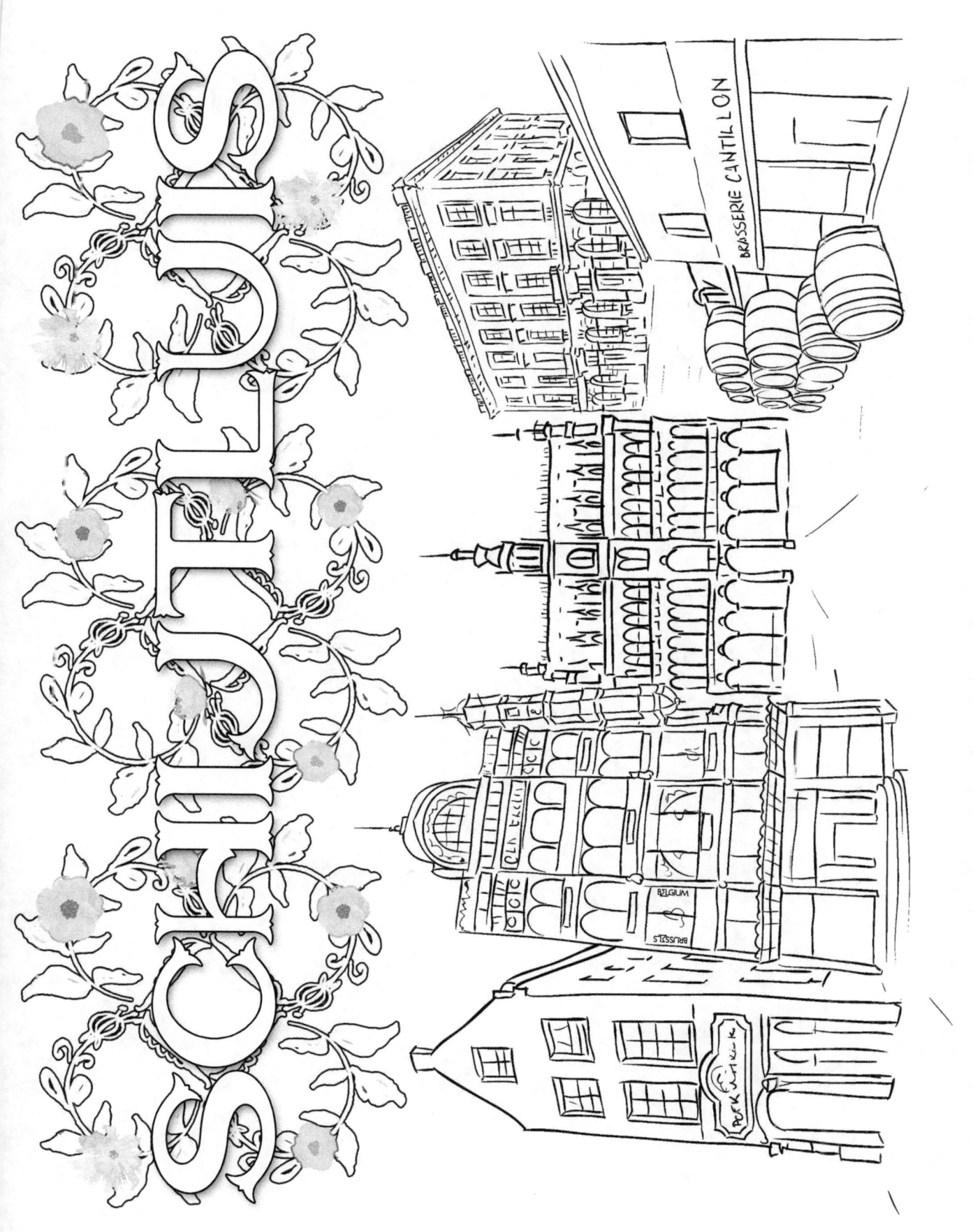

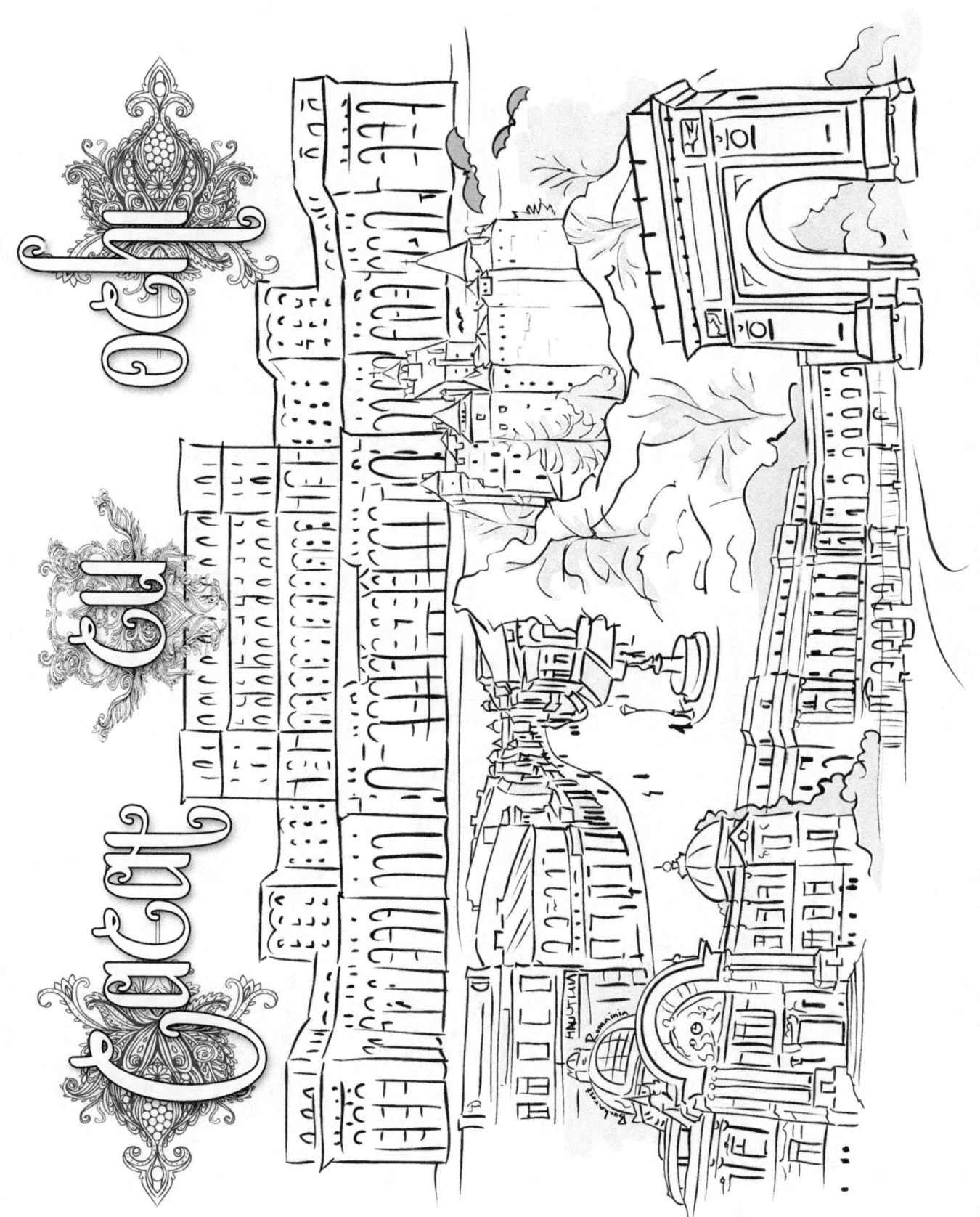

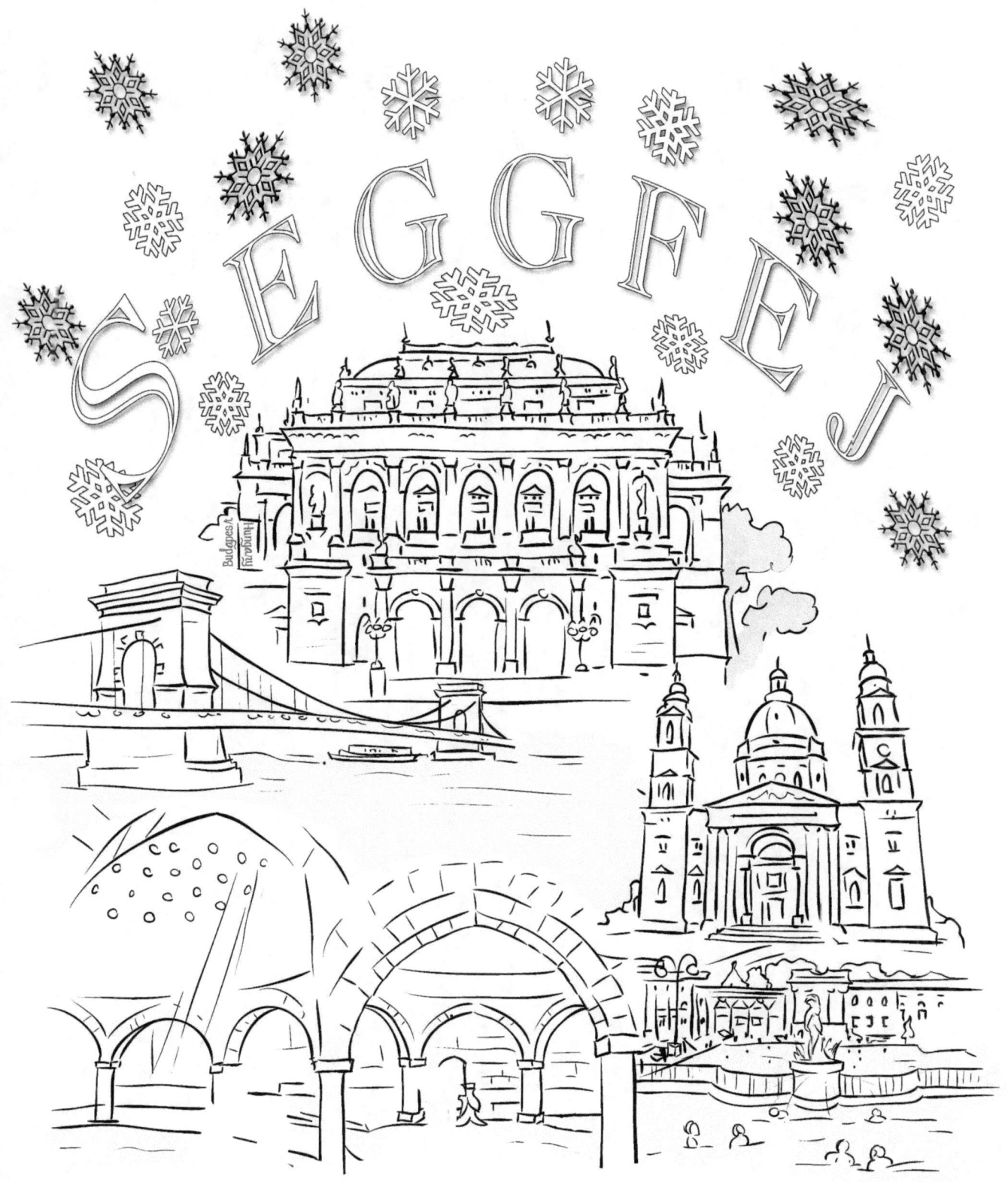

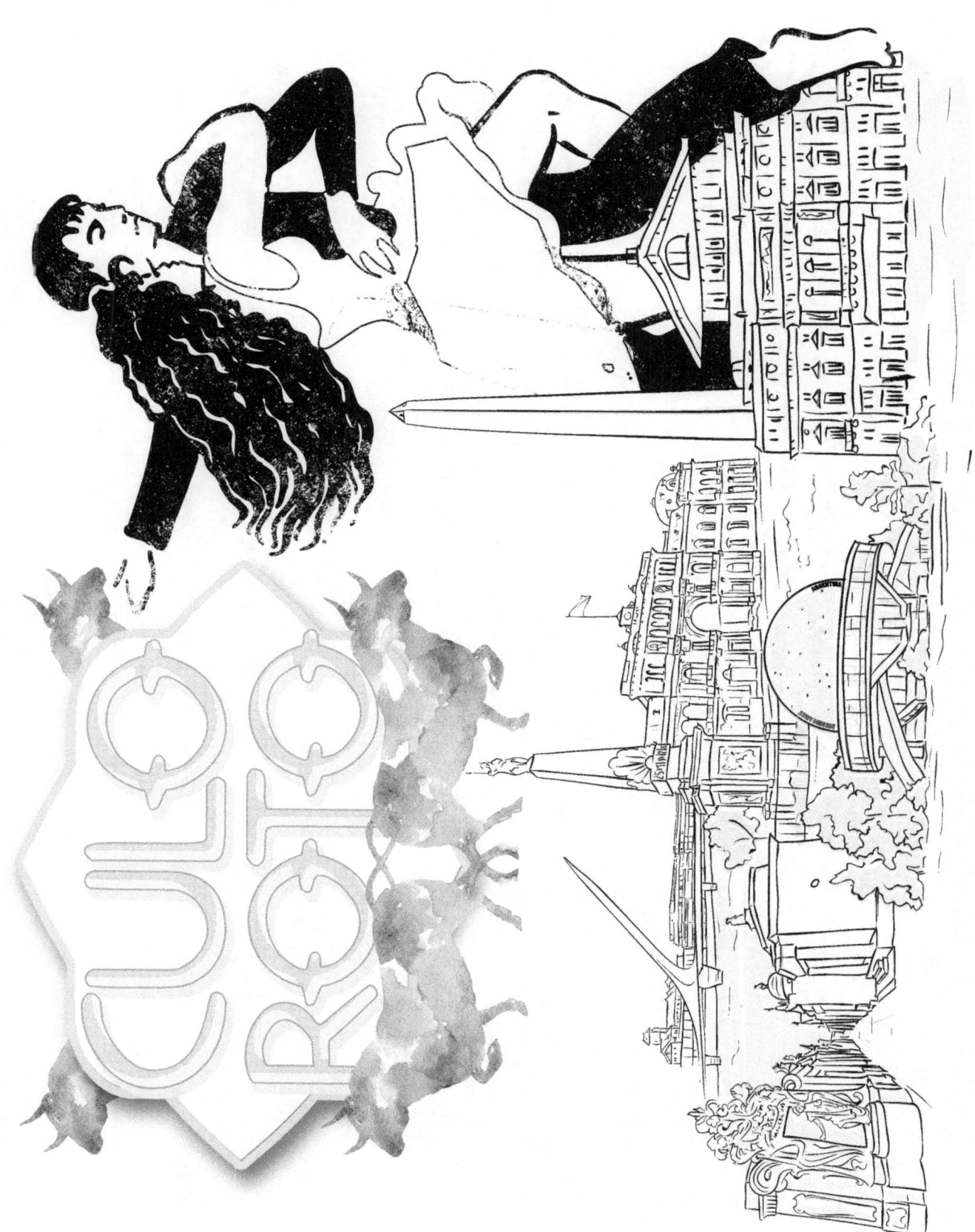

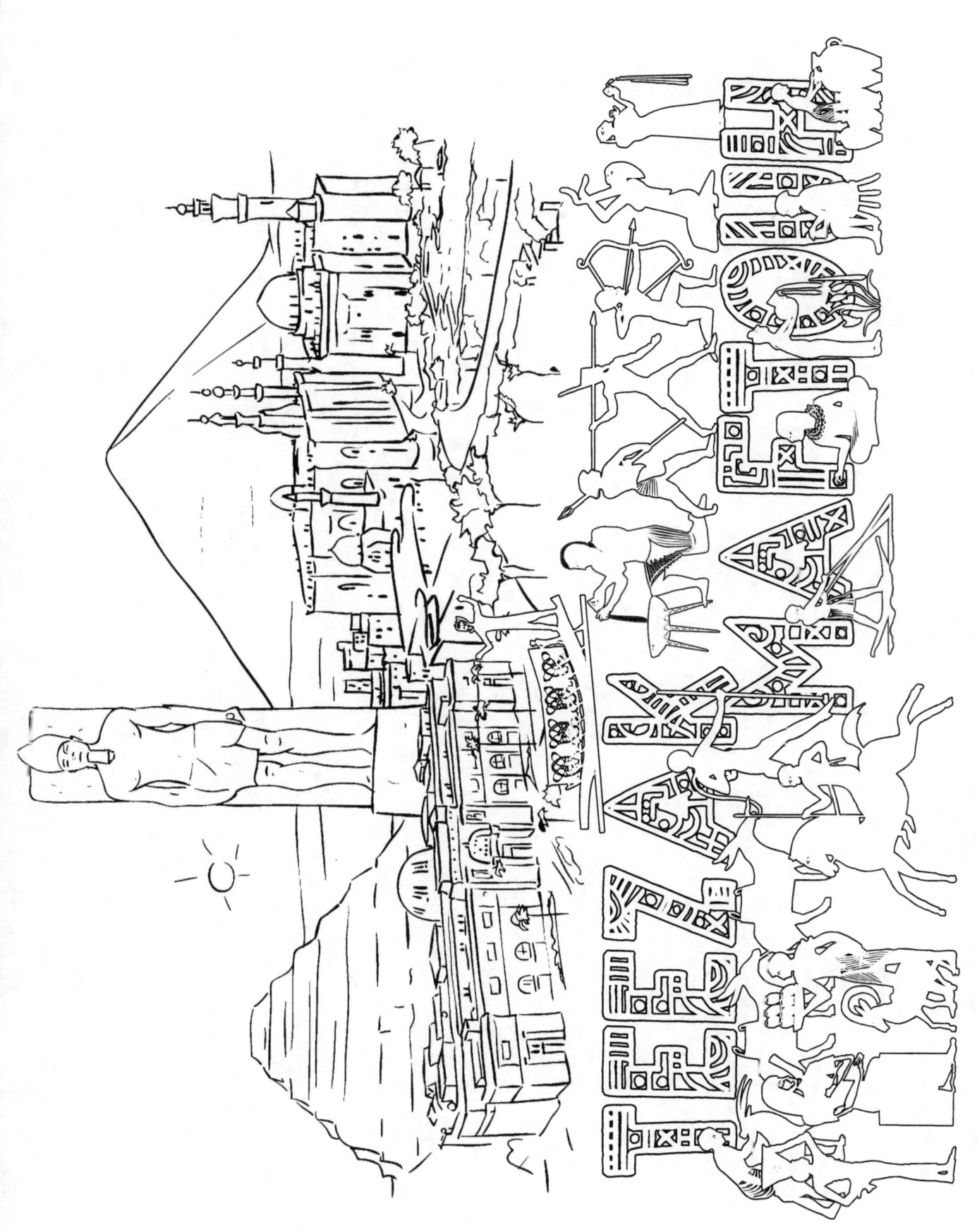

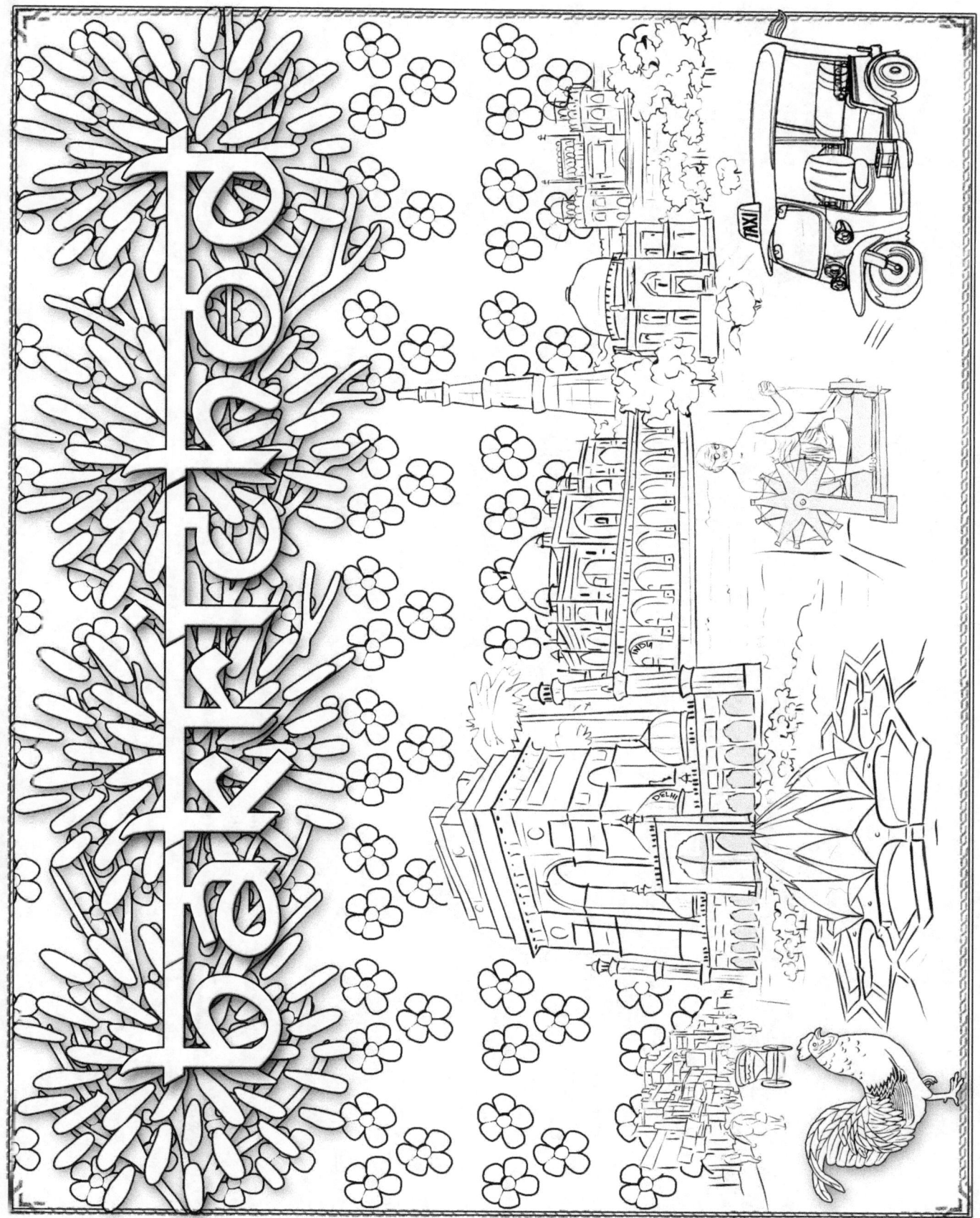

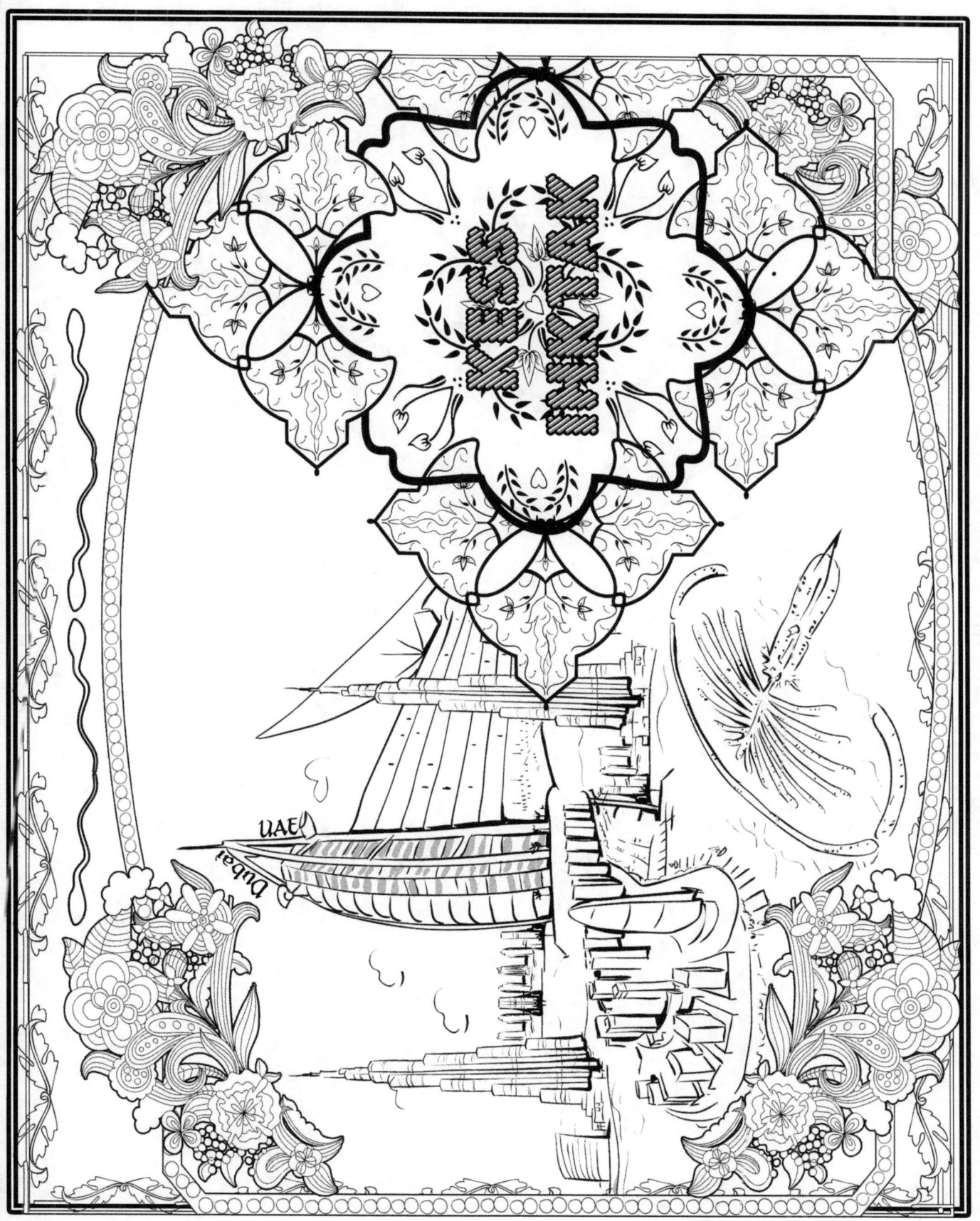

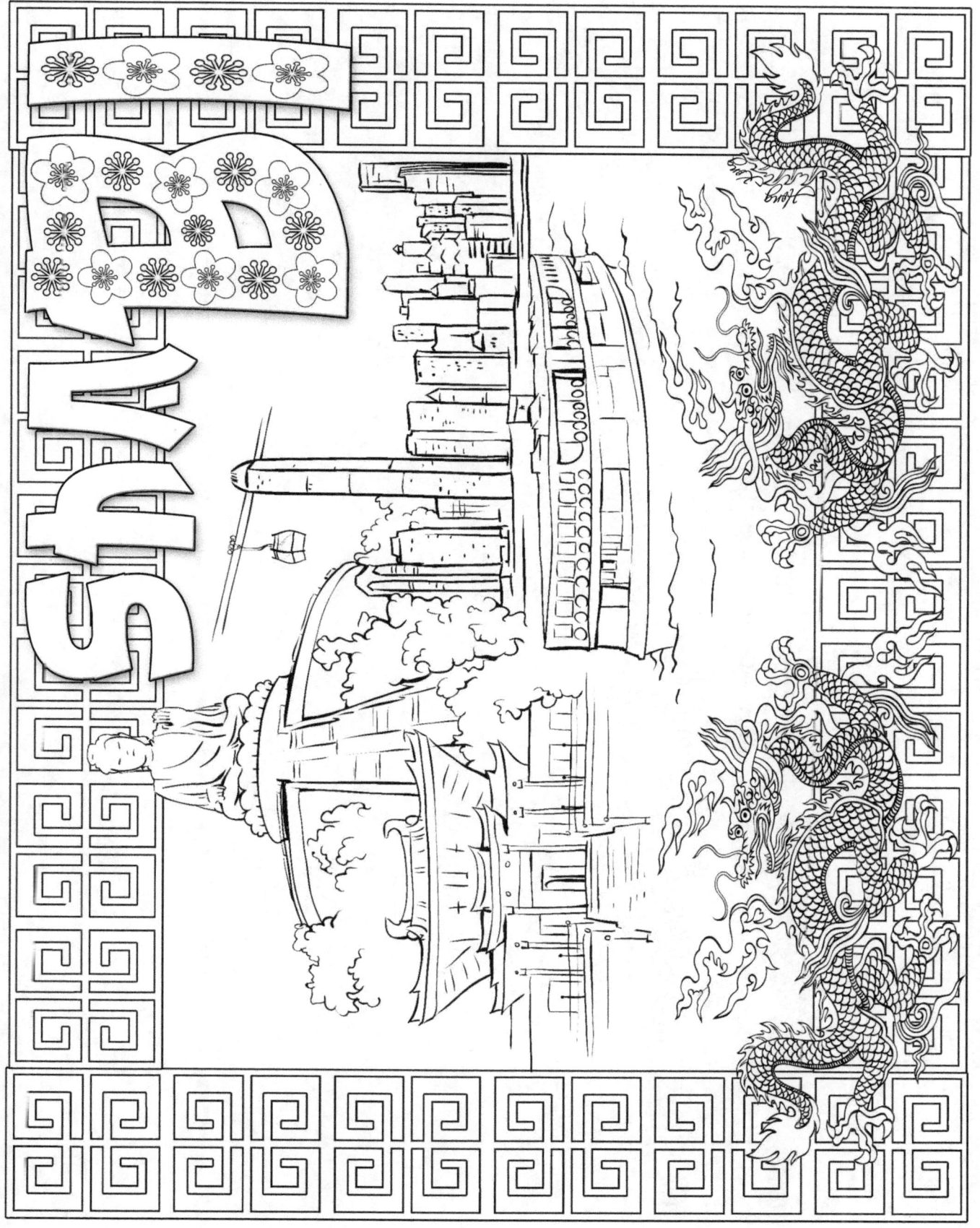

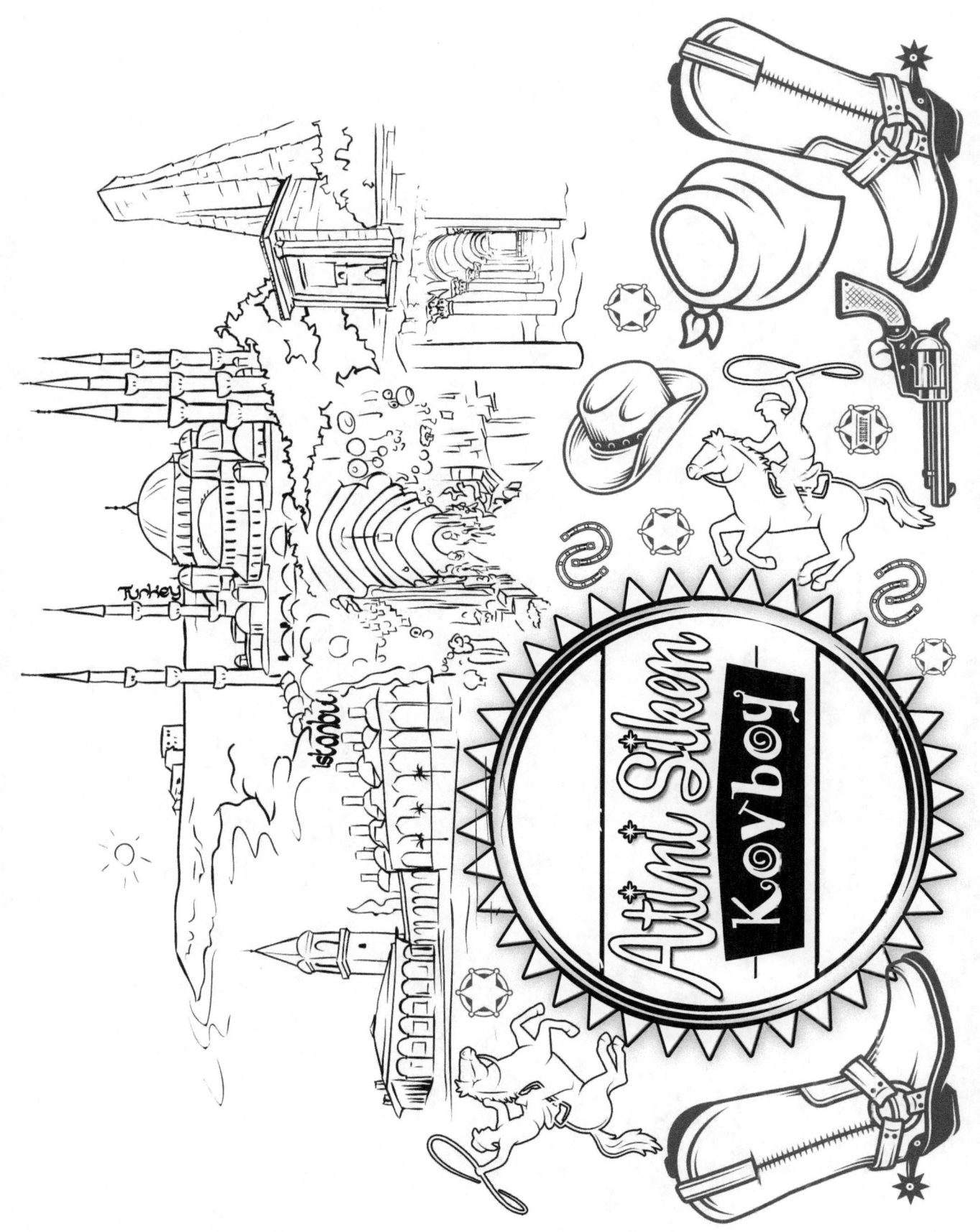

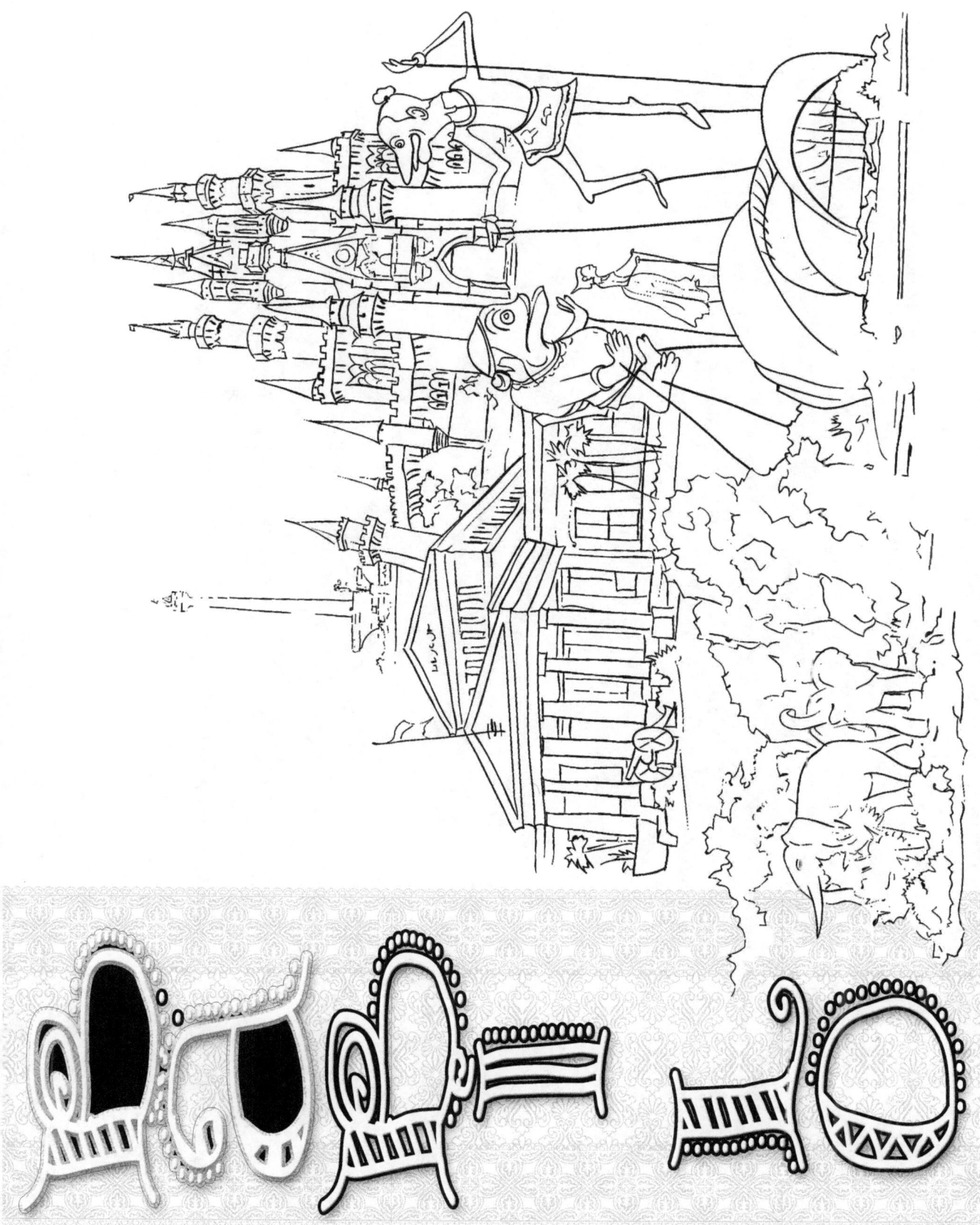

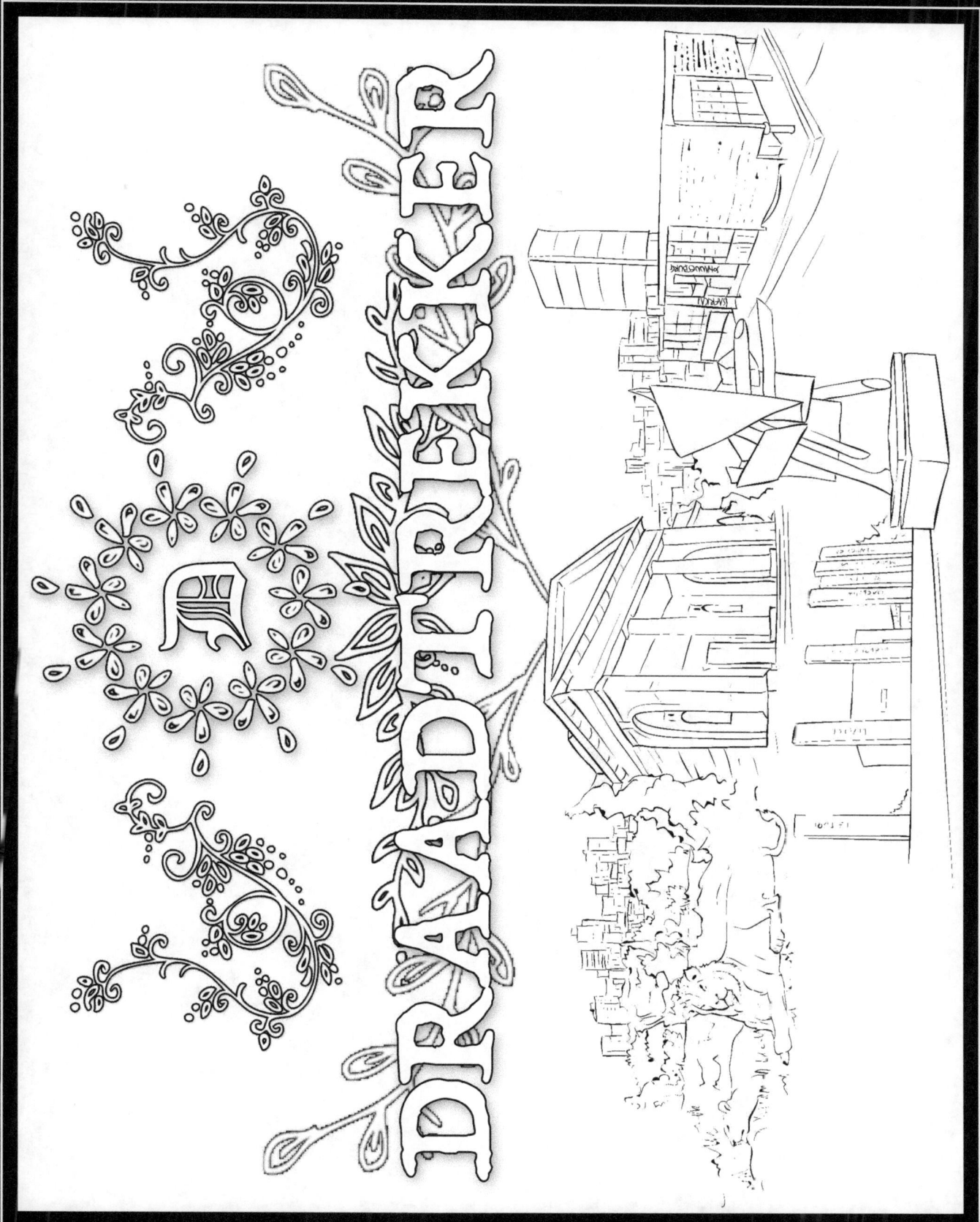

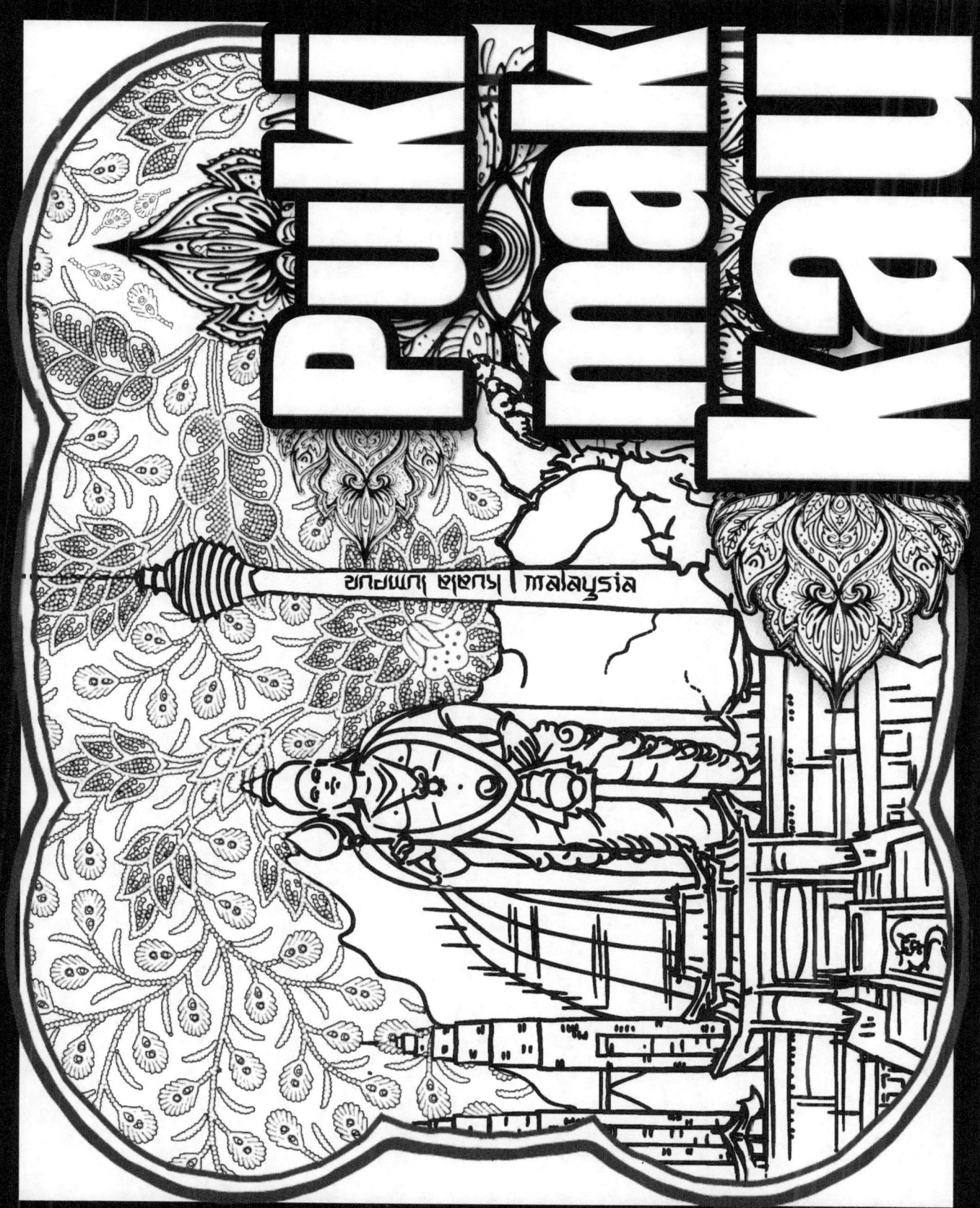

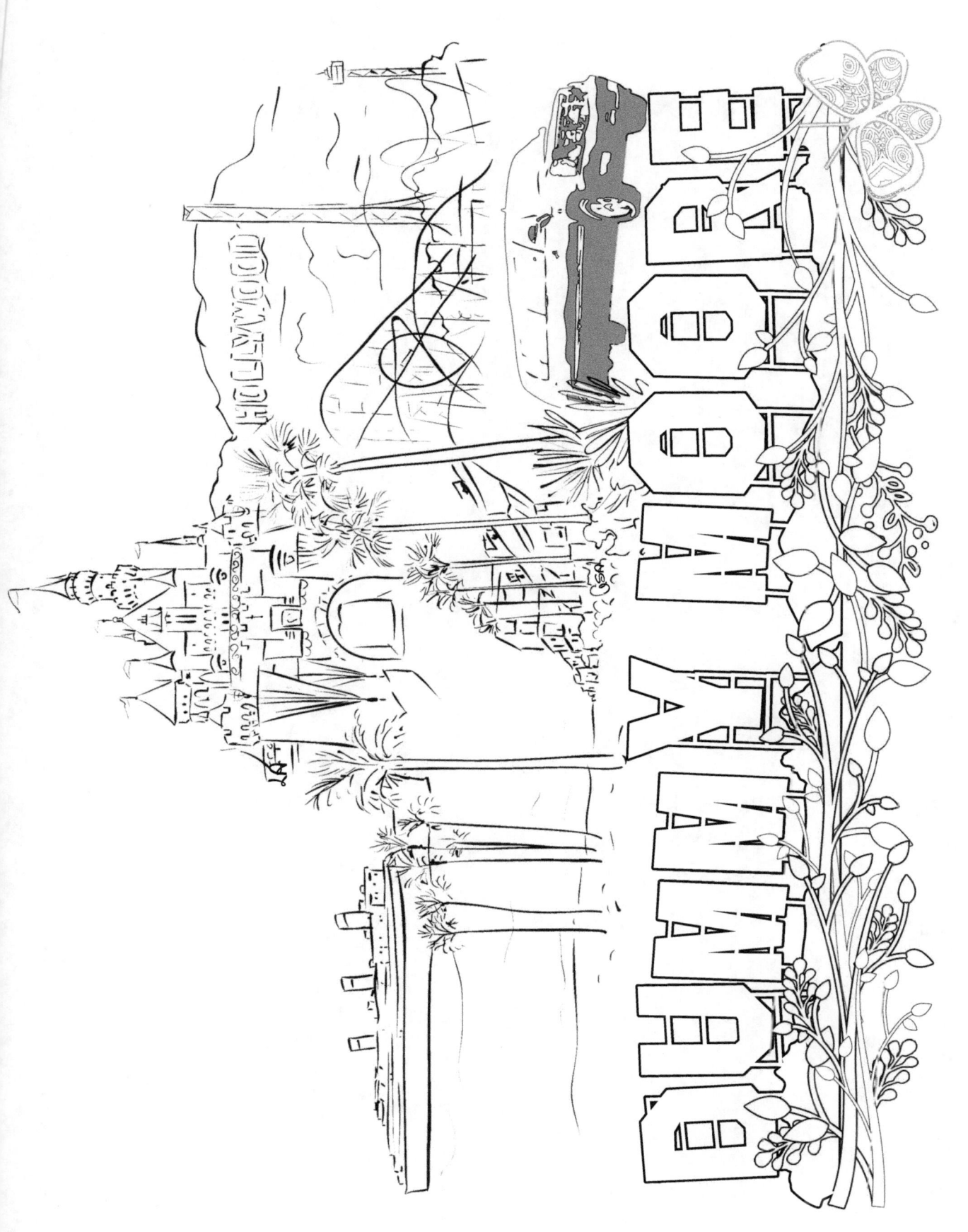

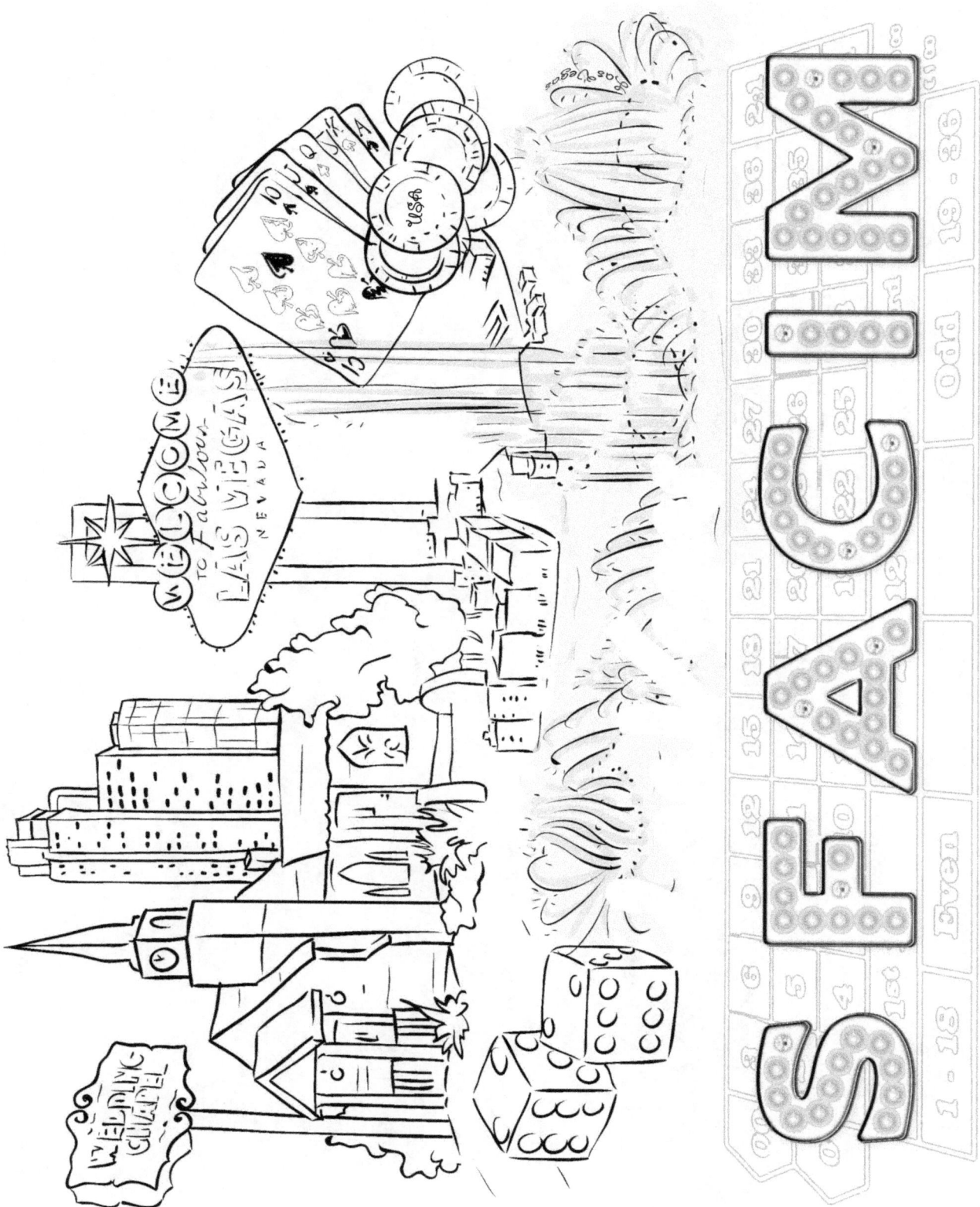

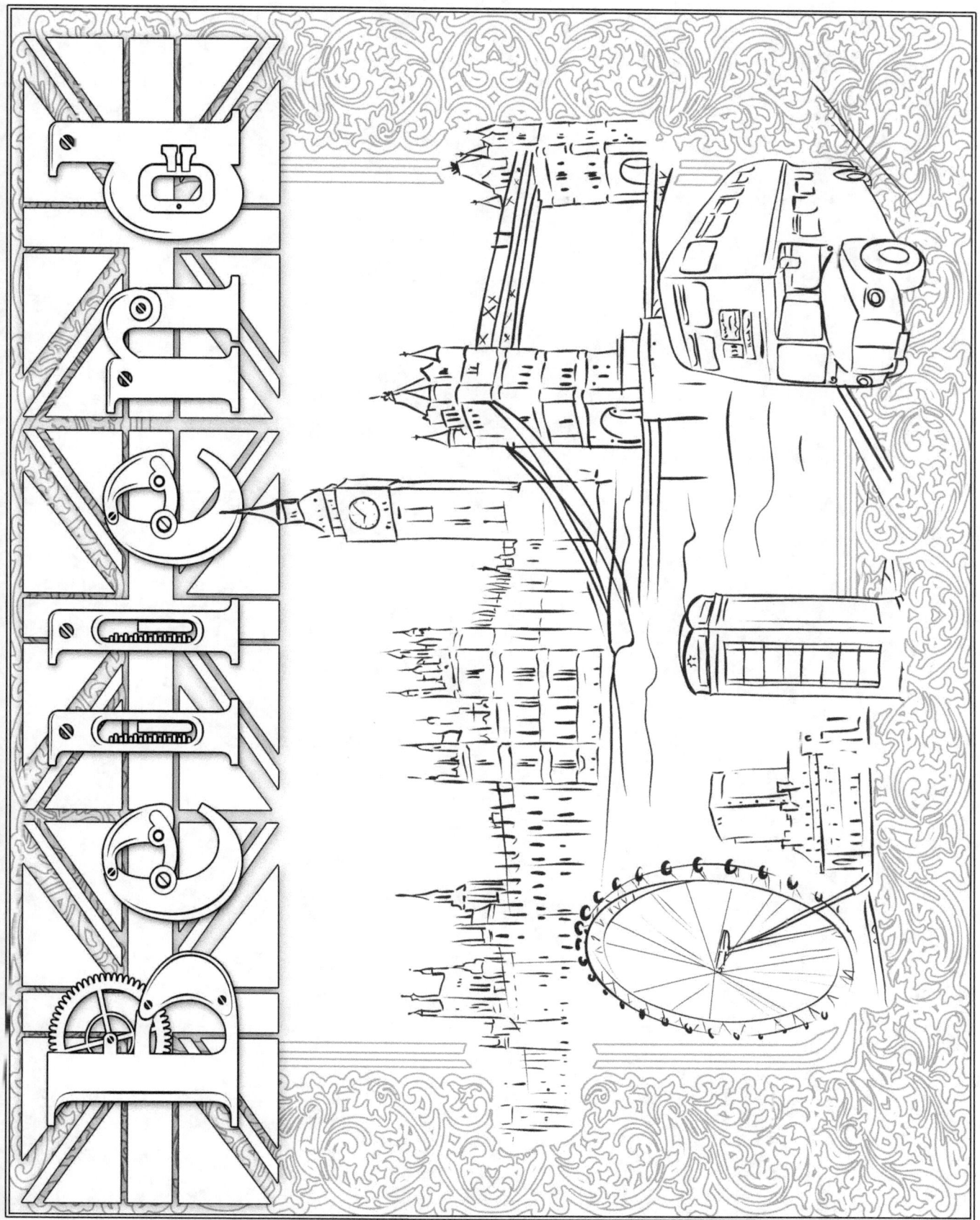

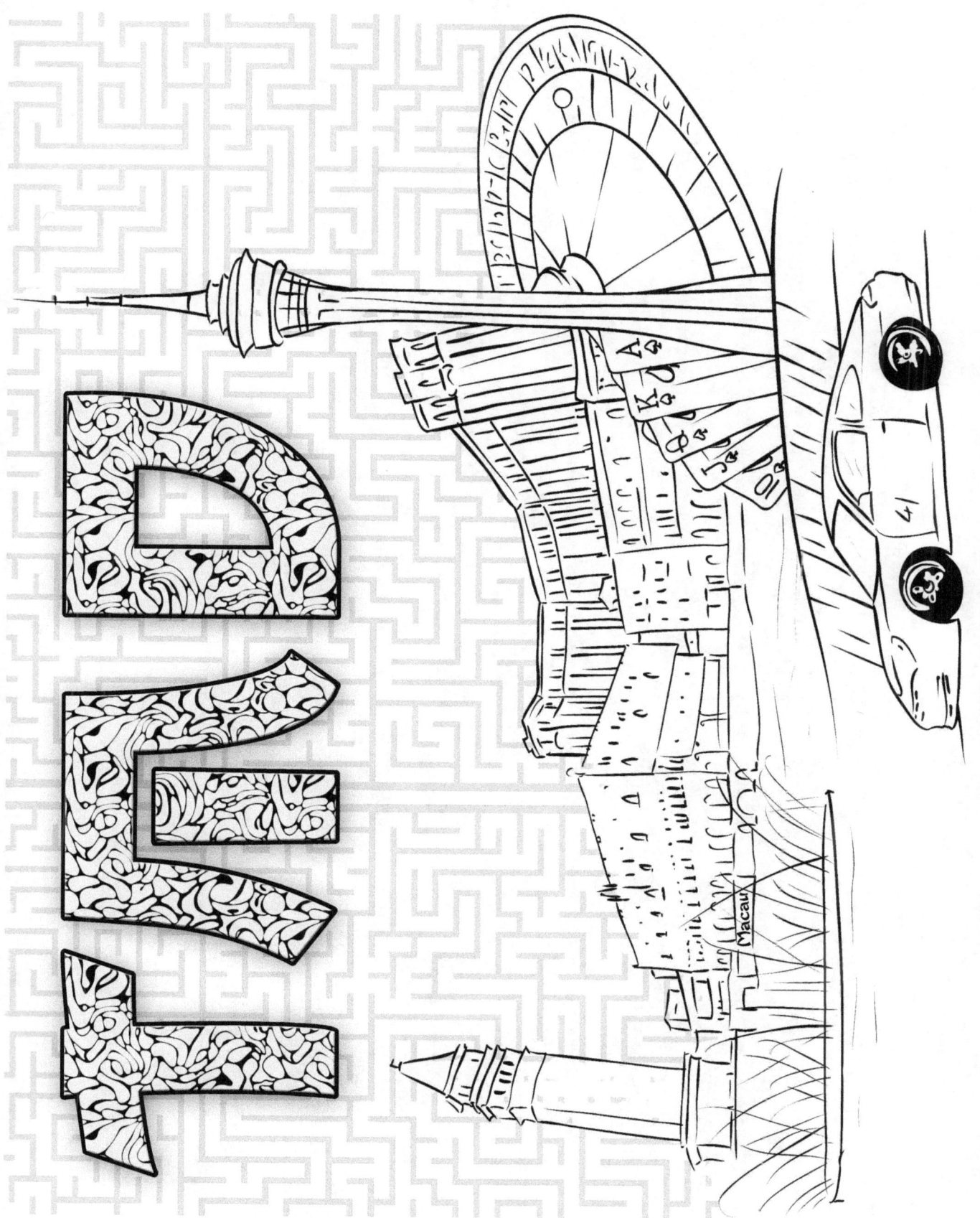

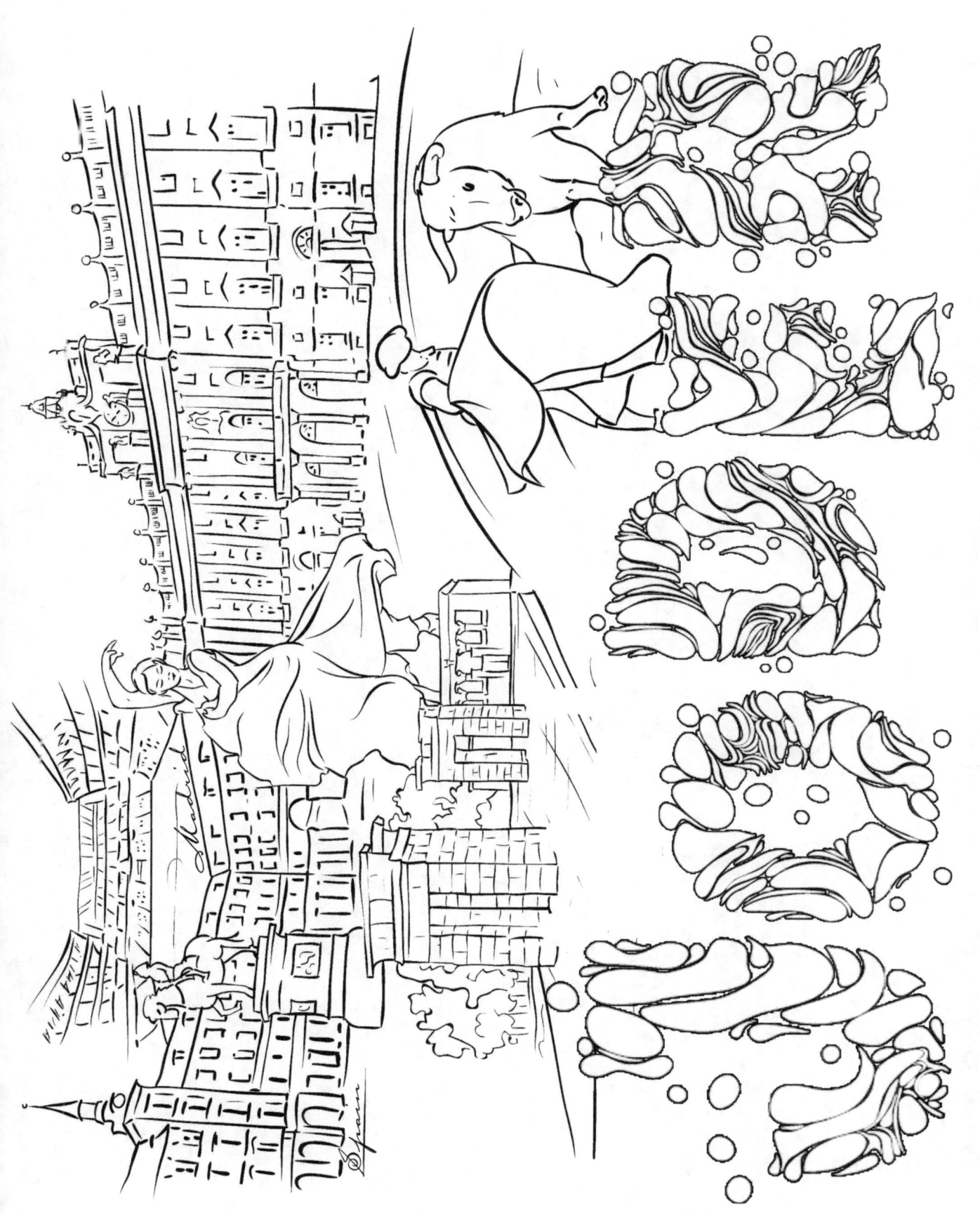

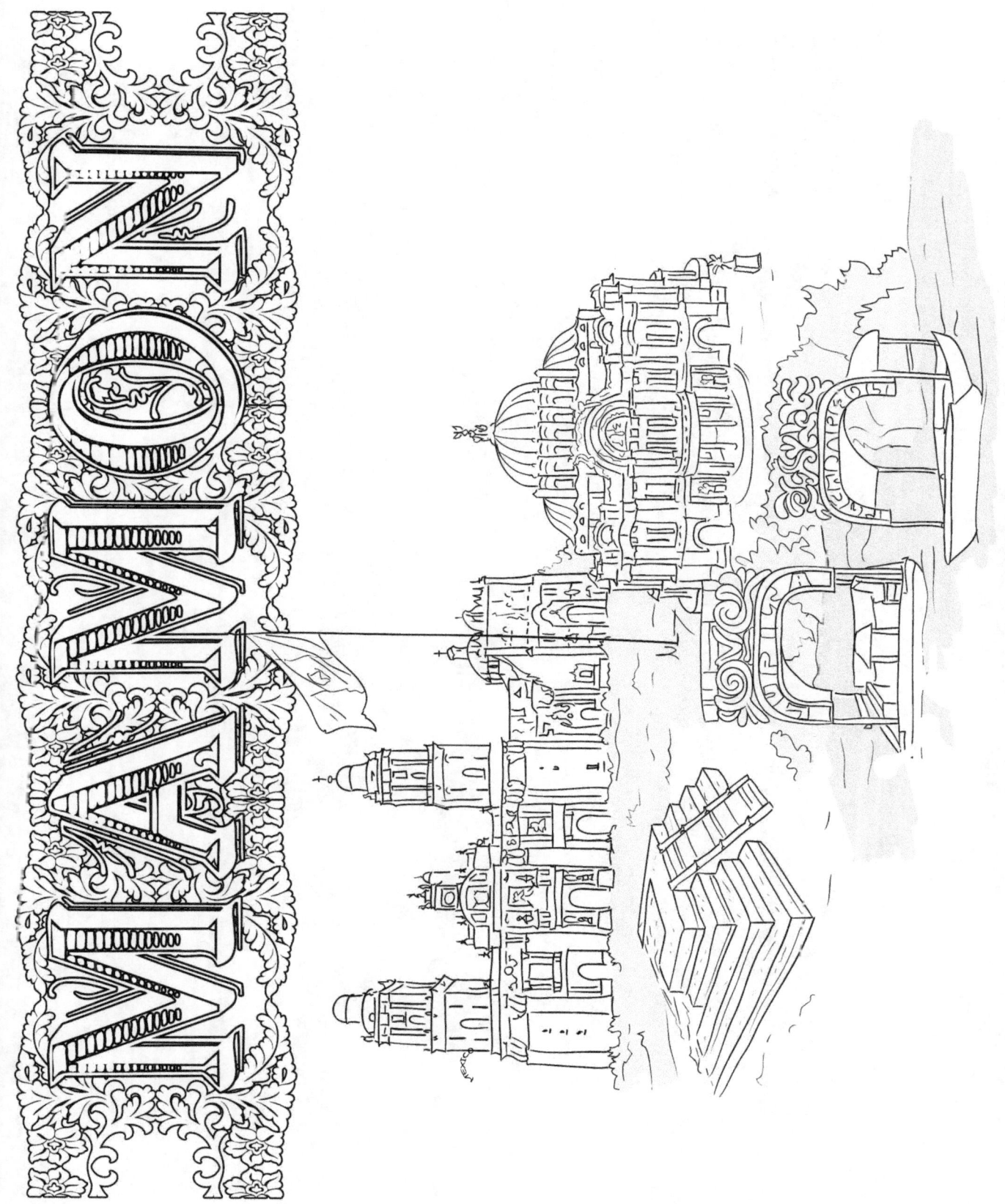

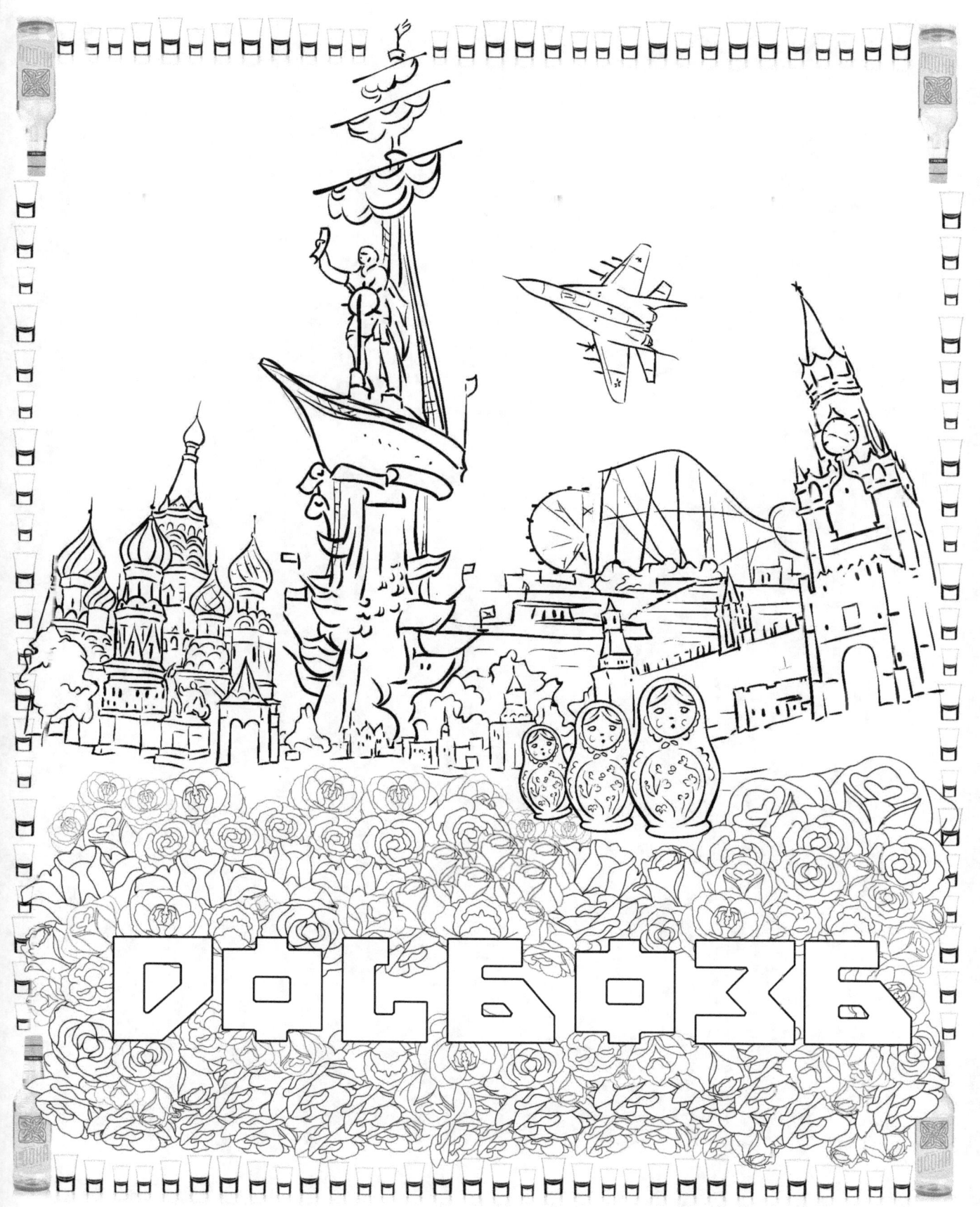

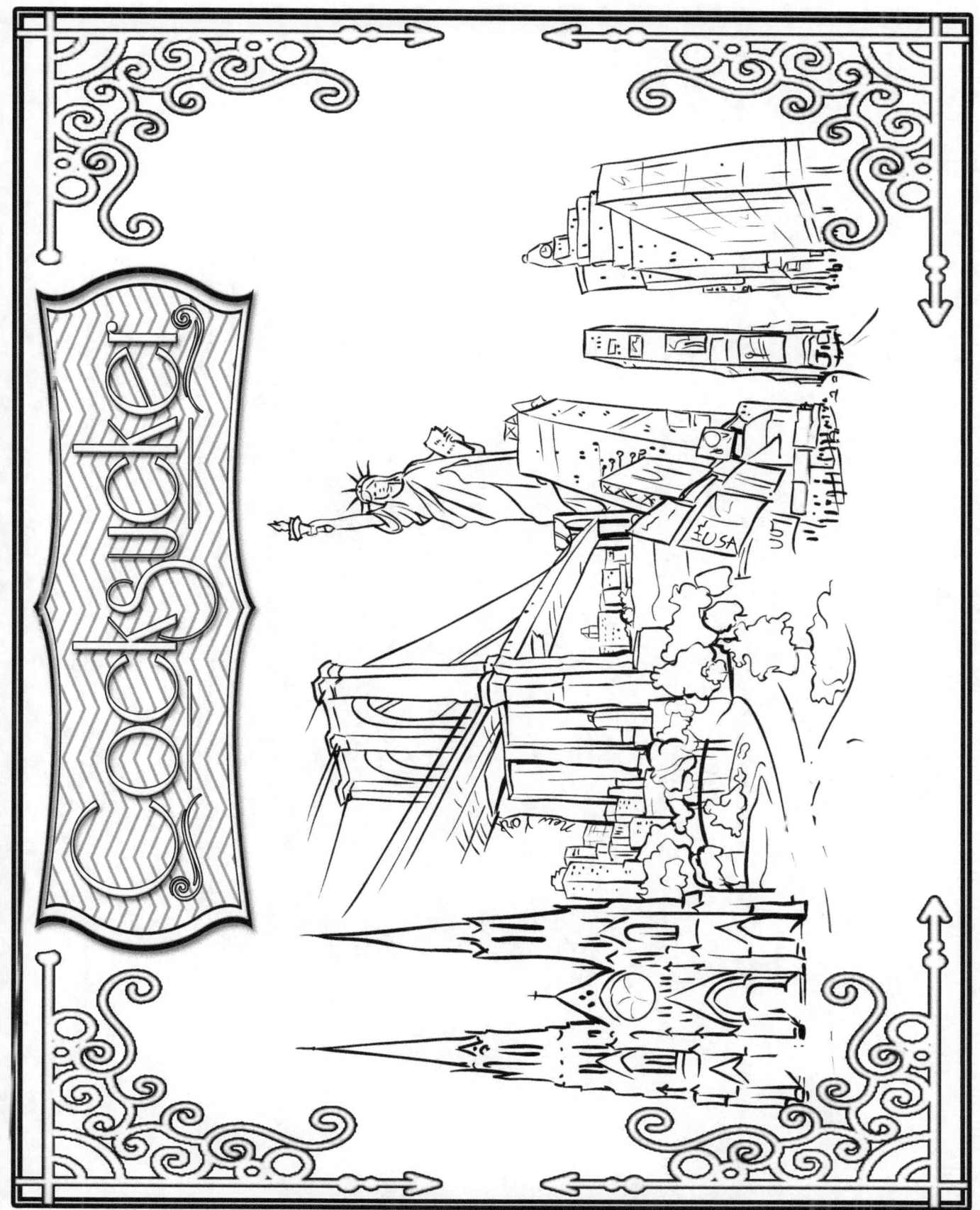

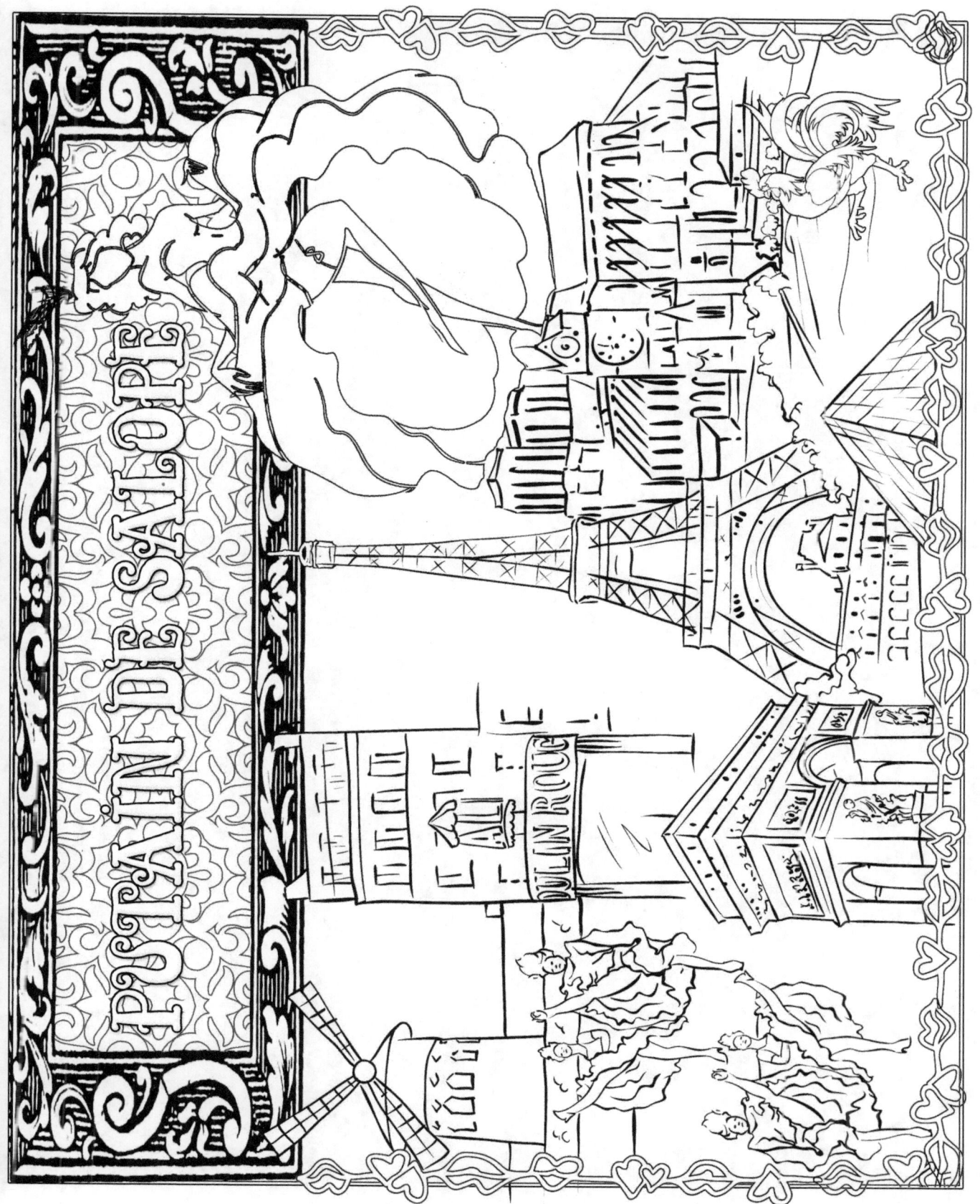

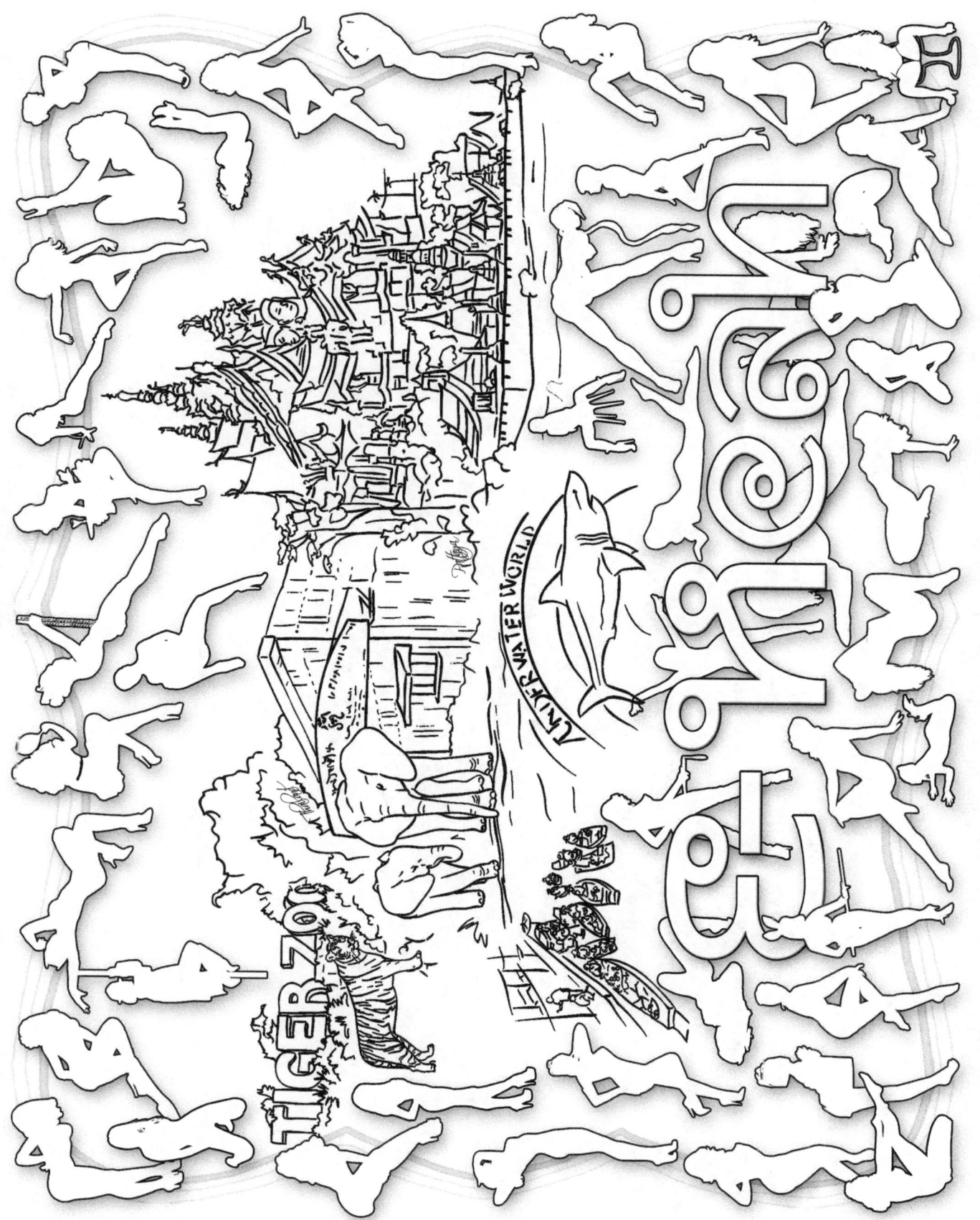

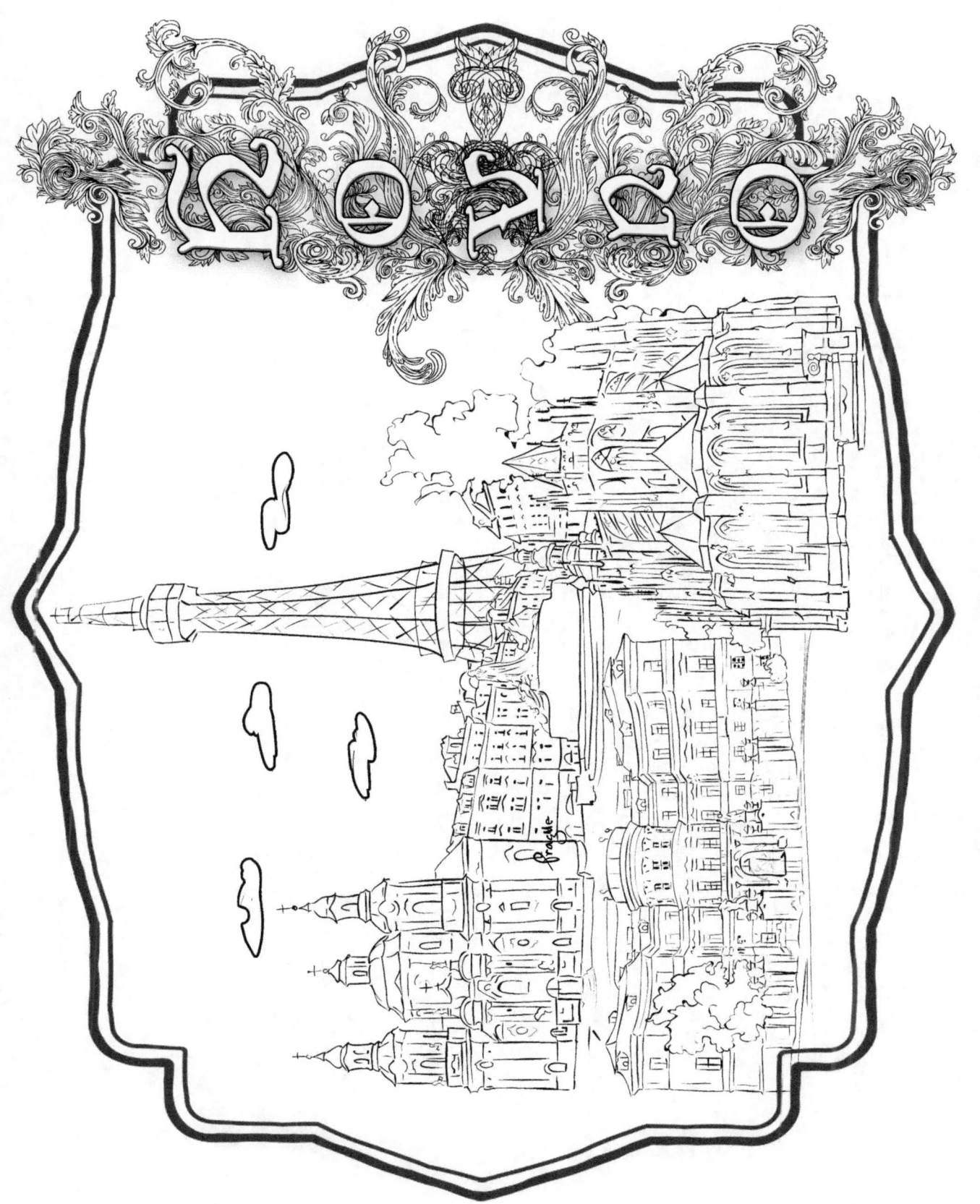

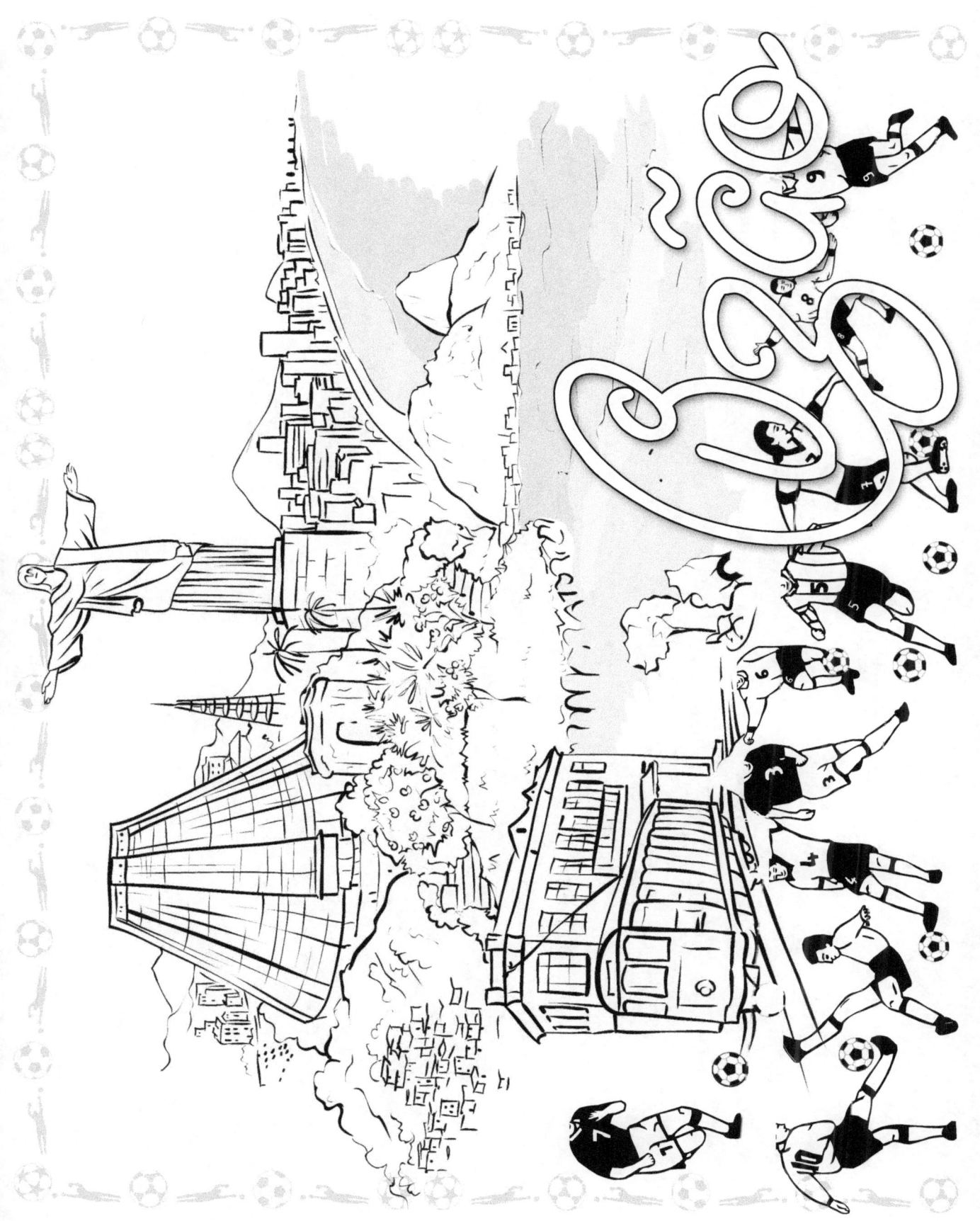

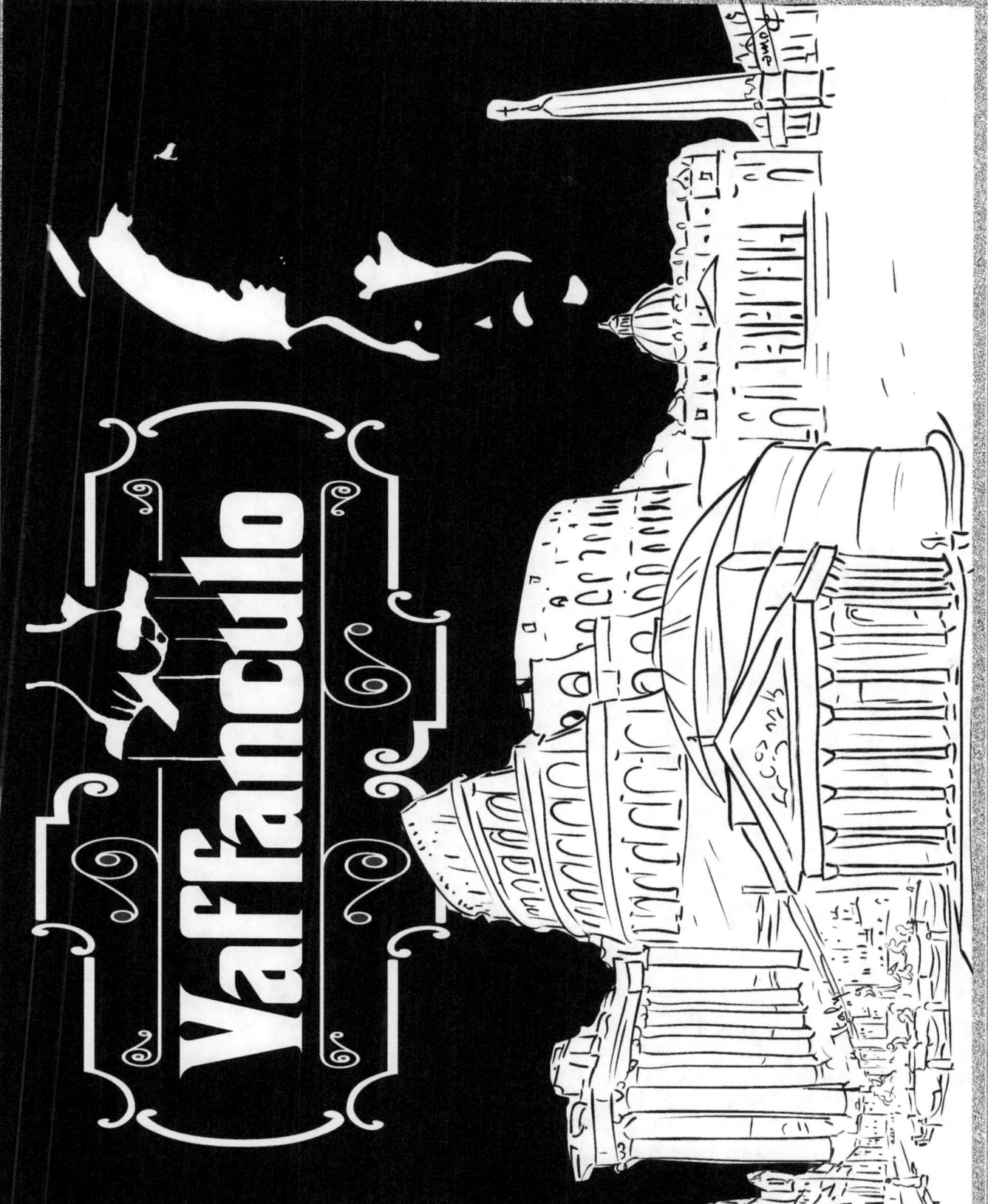

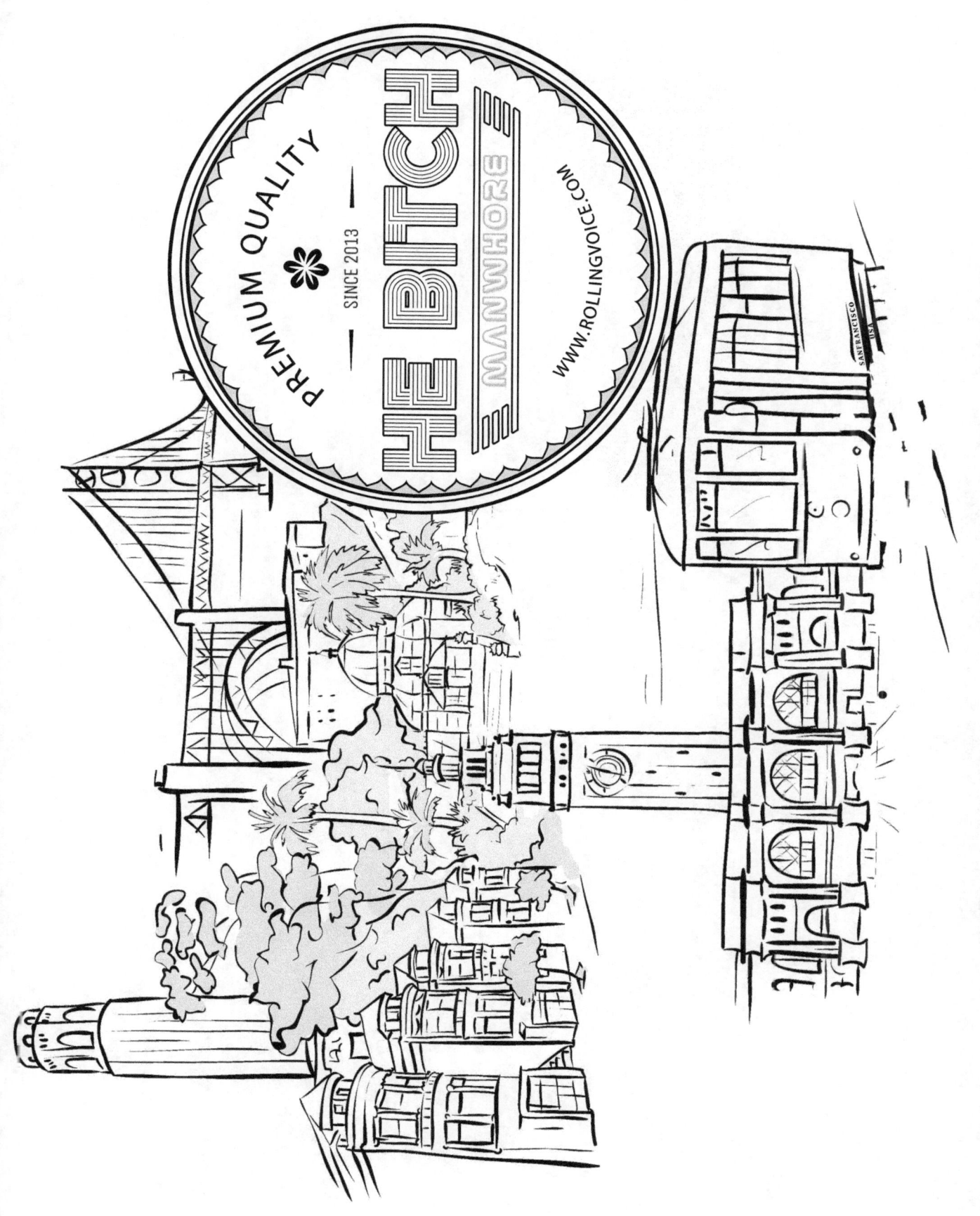

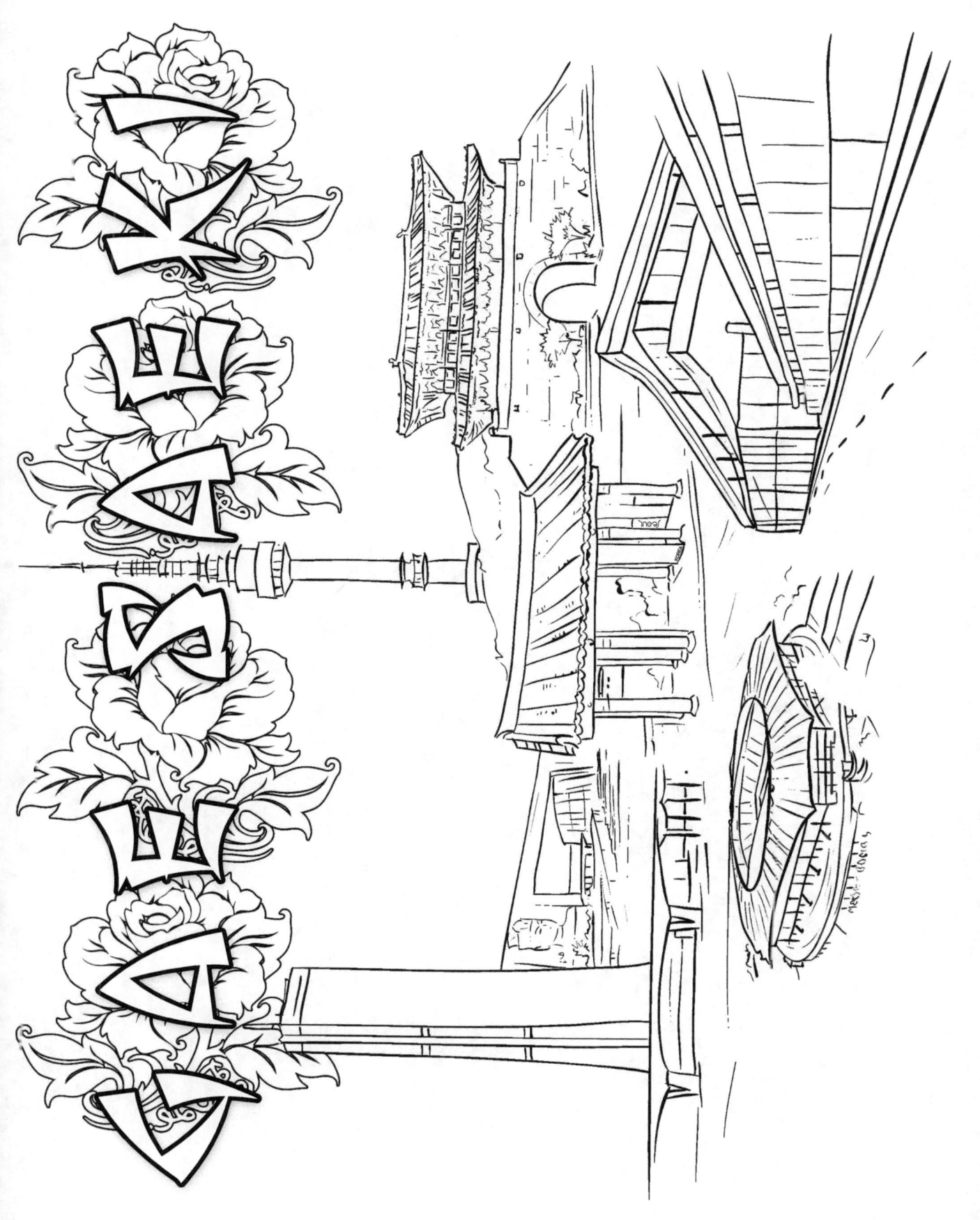

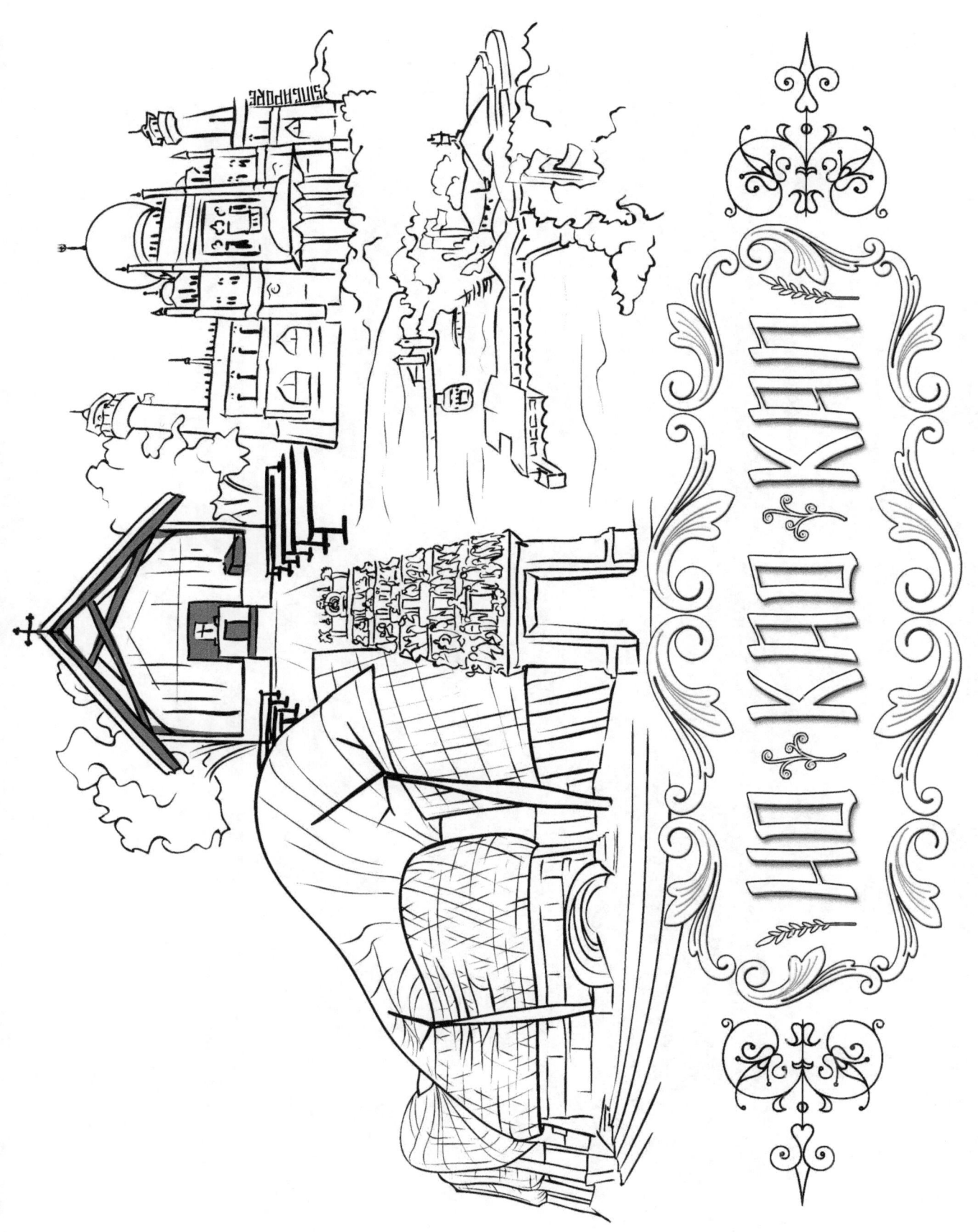

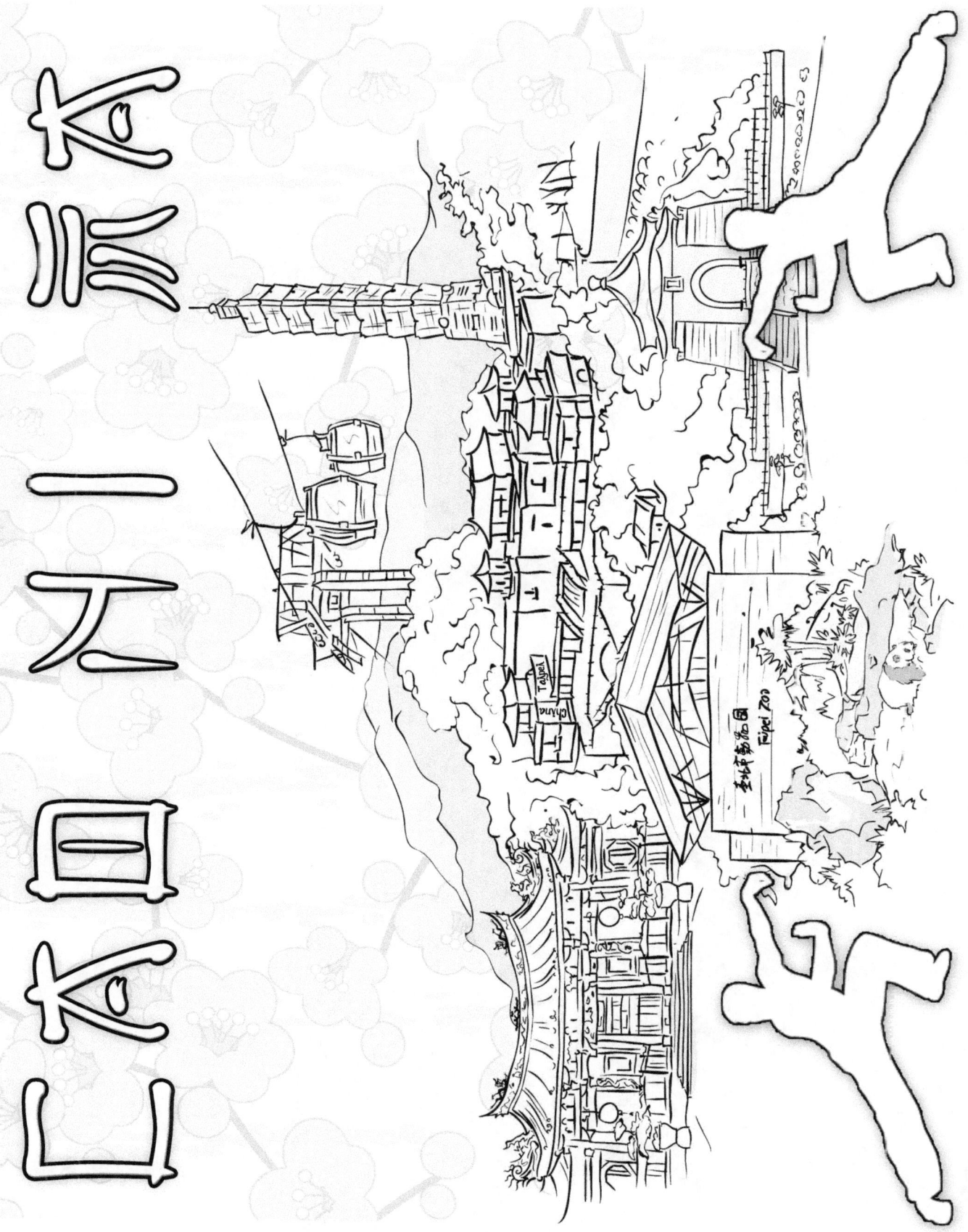

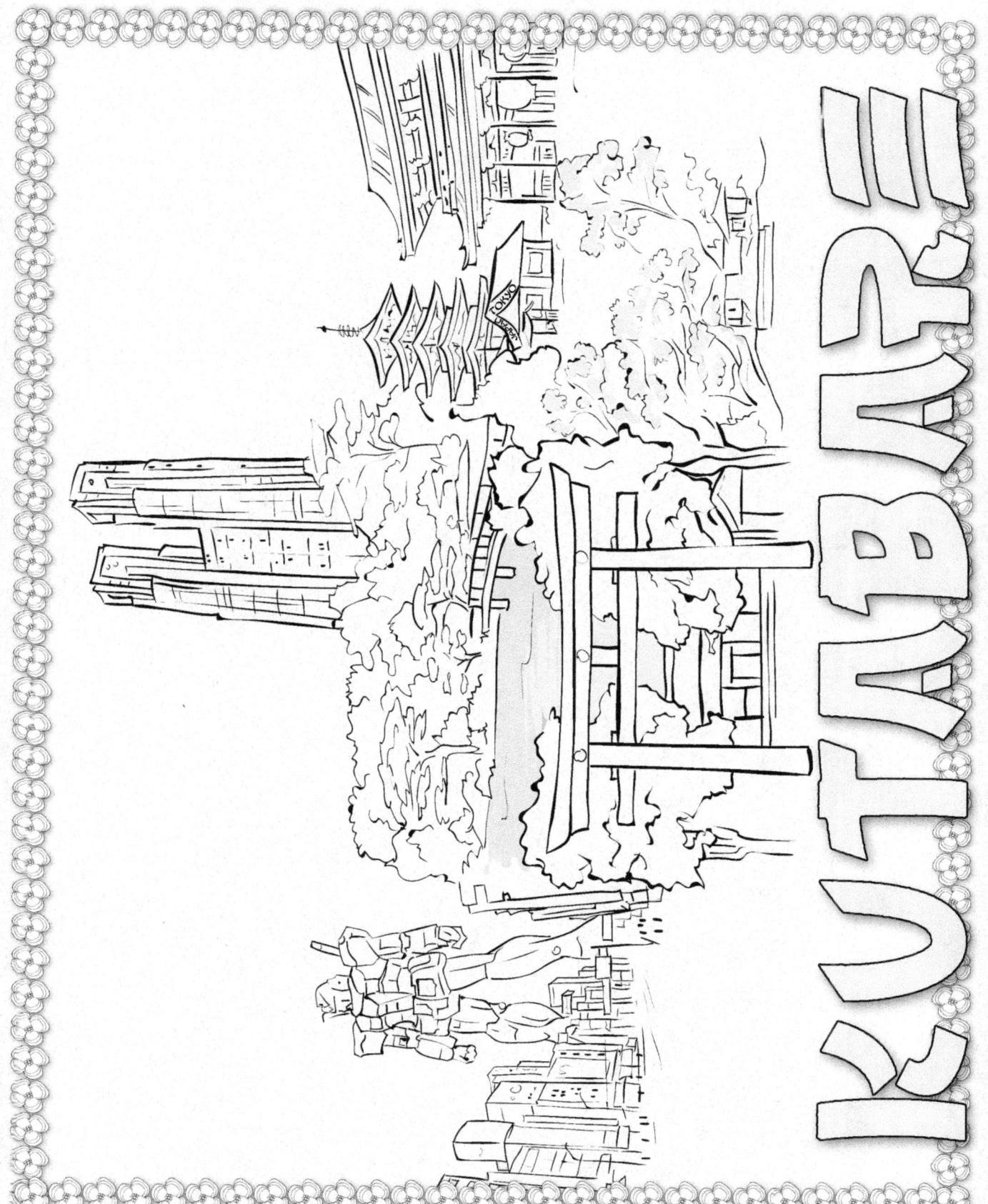

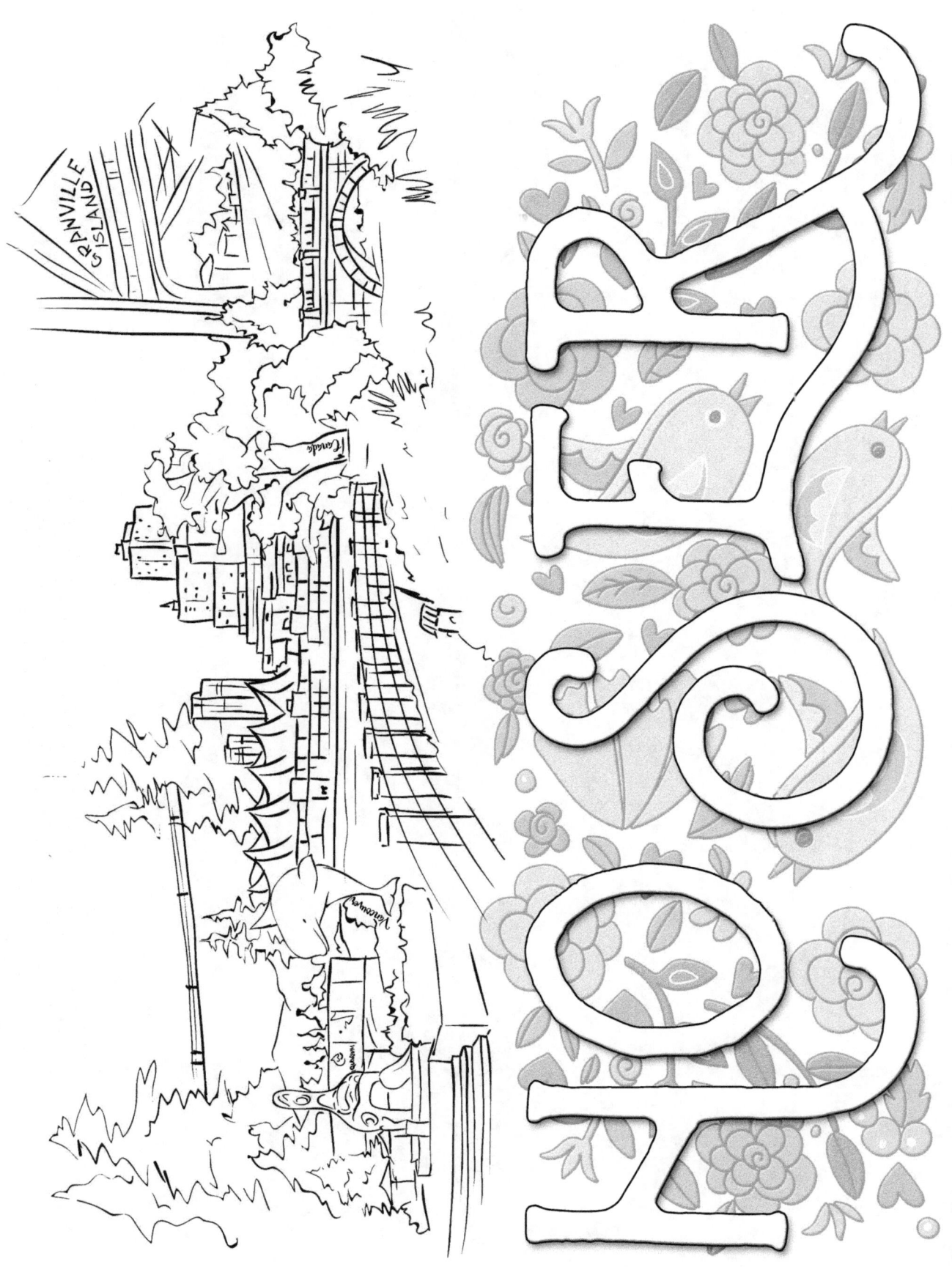

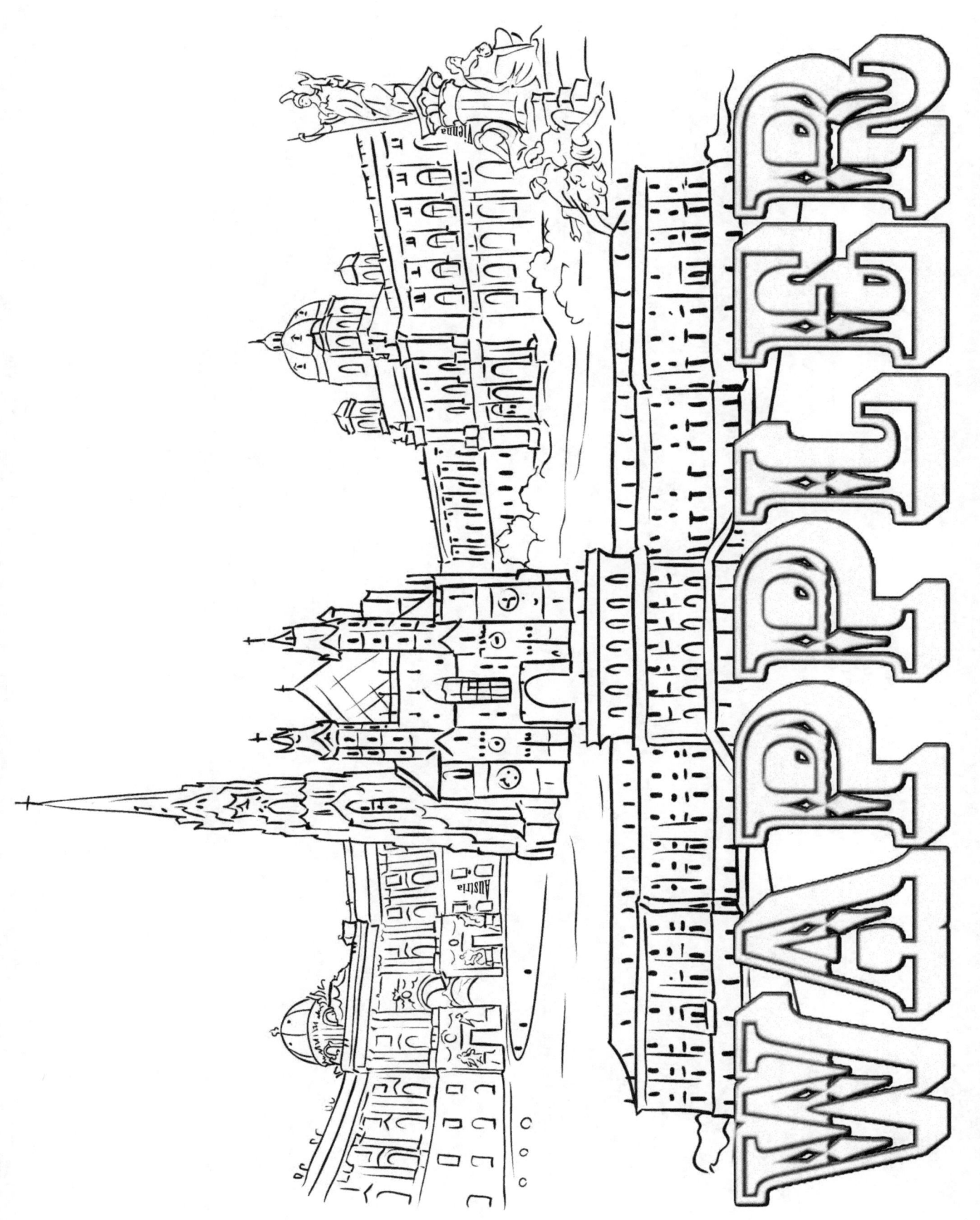

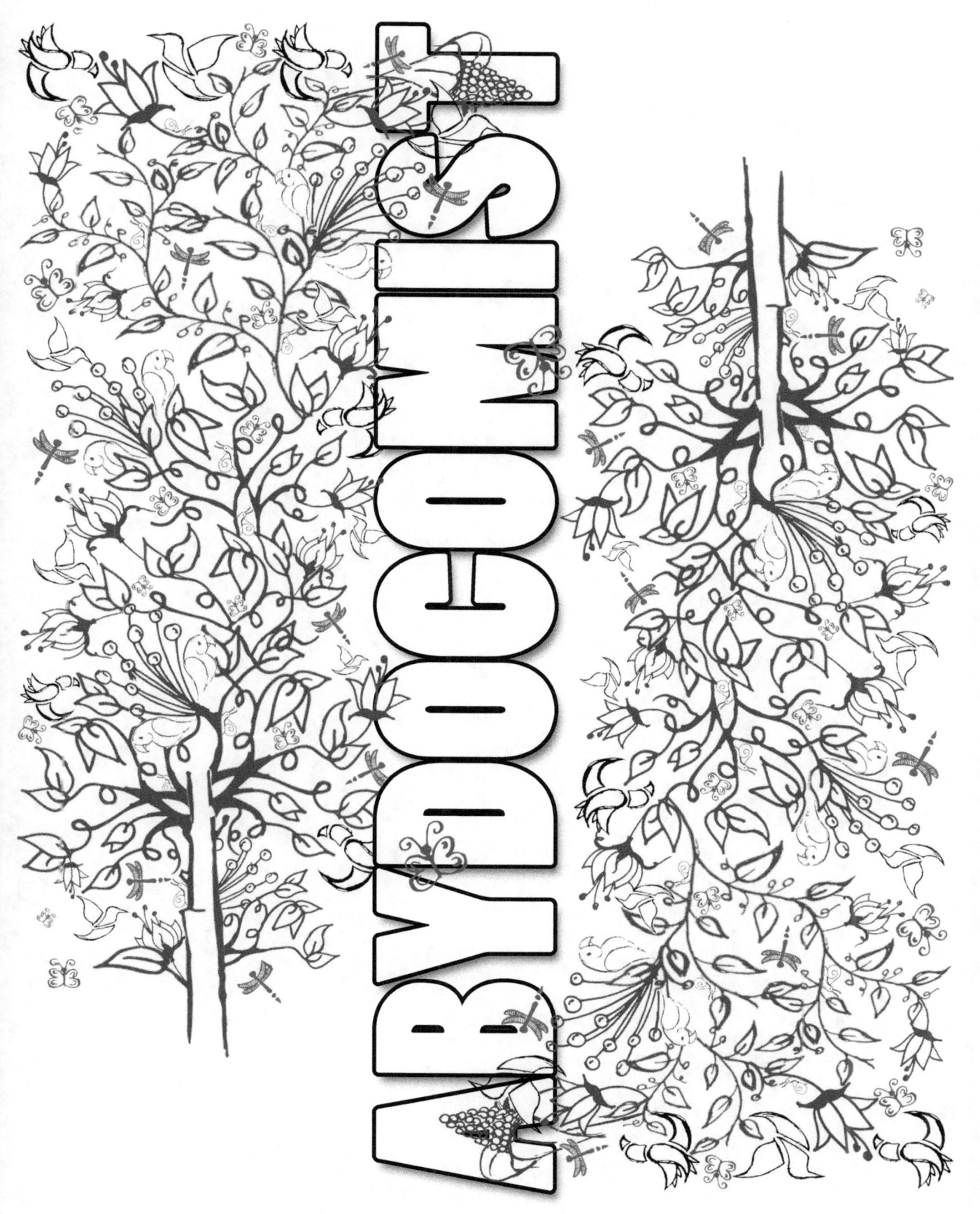

Beardsplitter

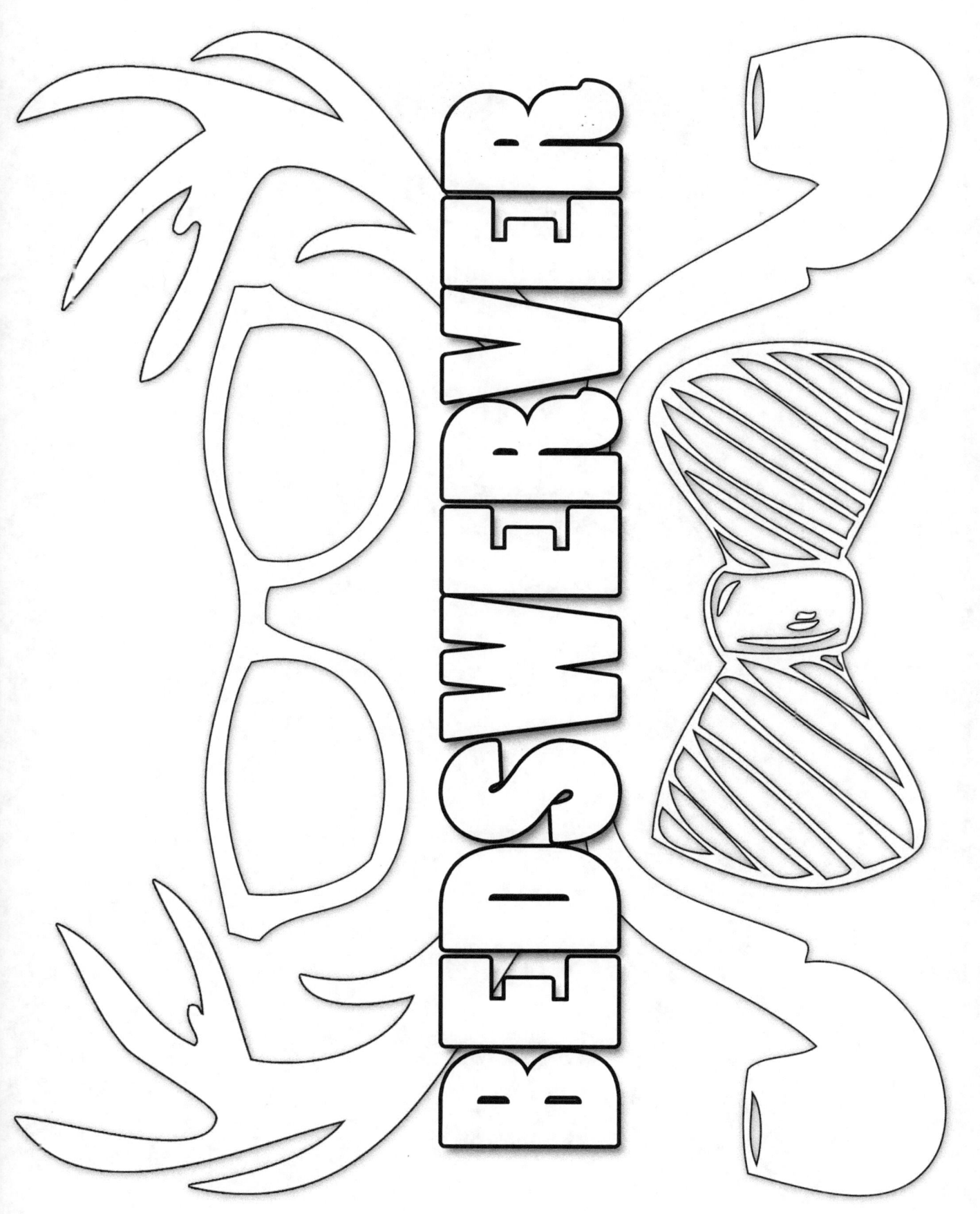

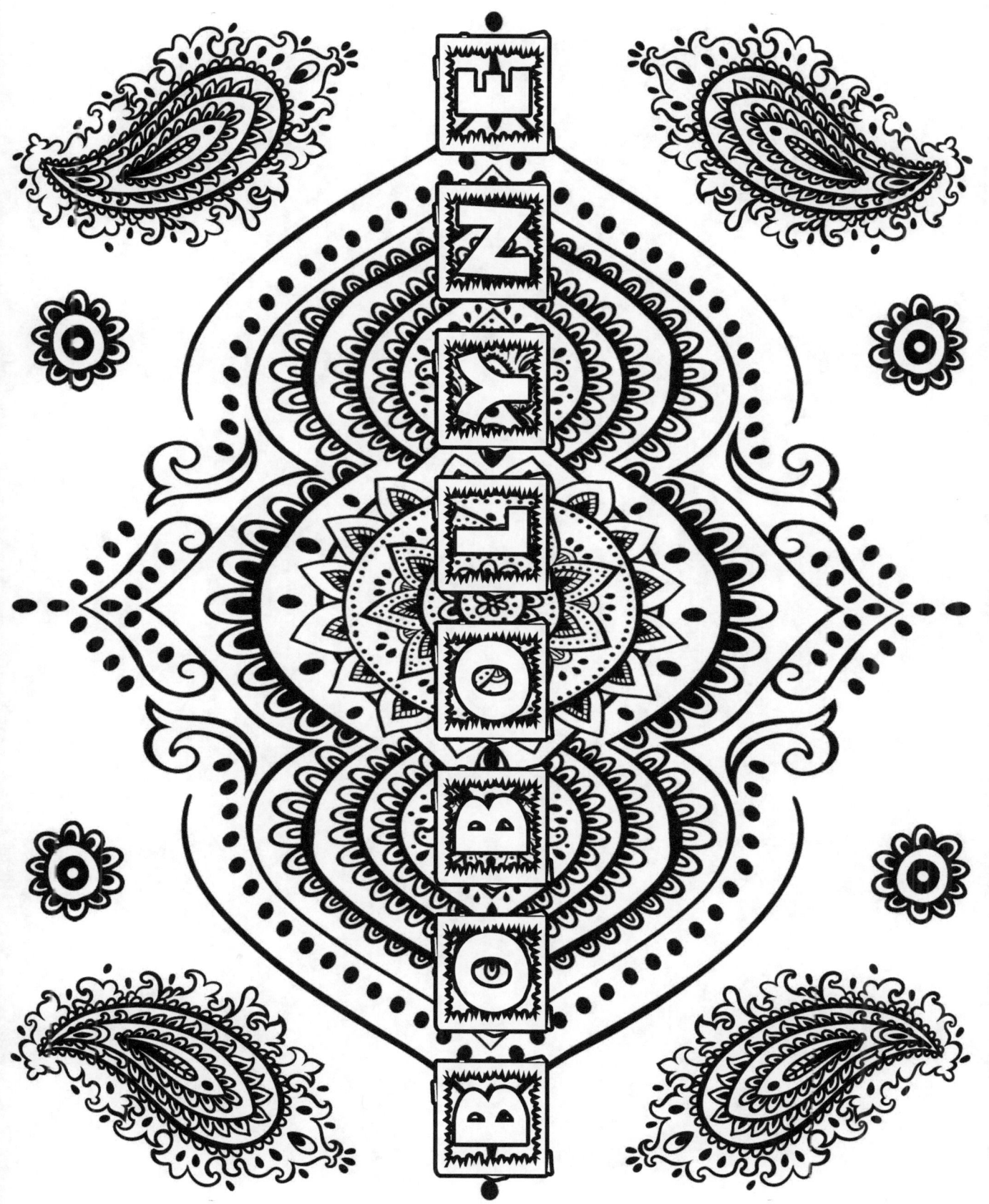

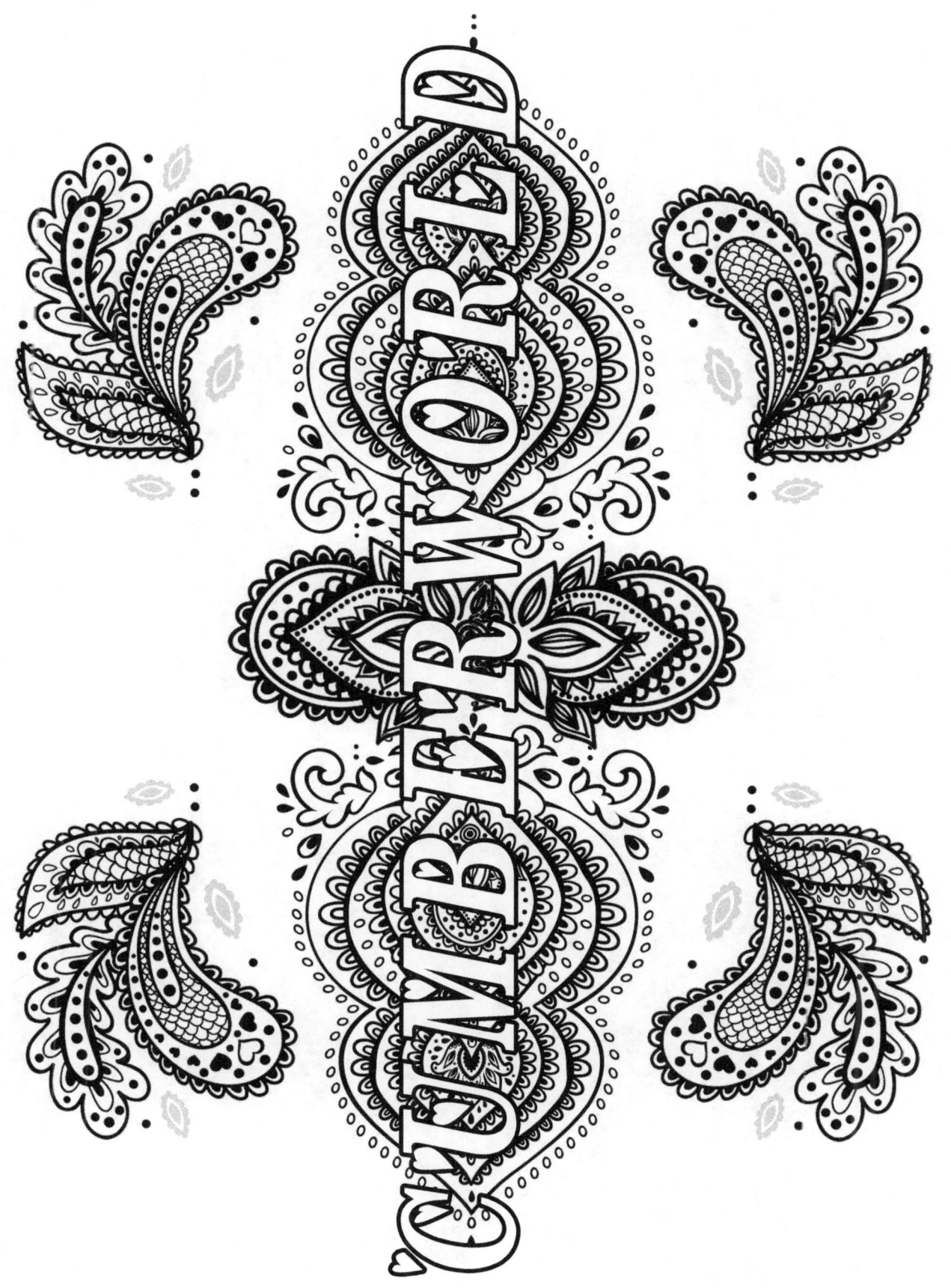

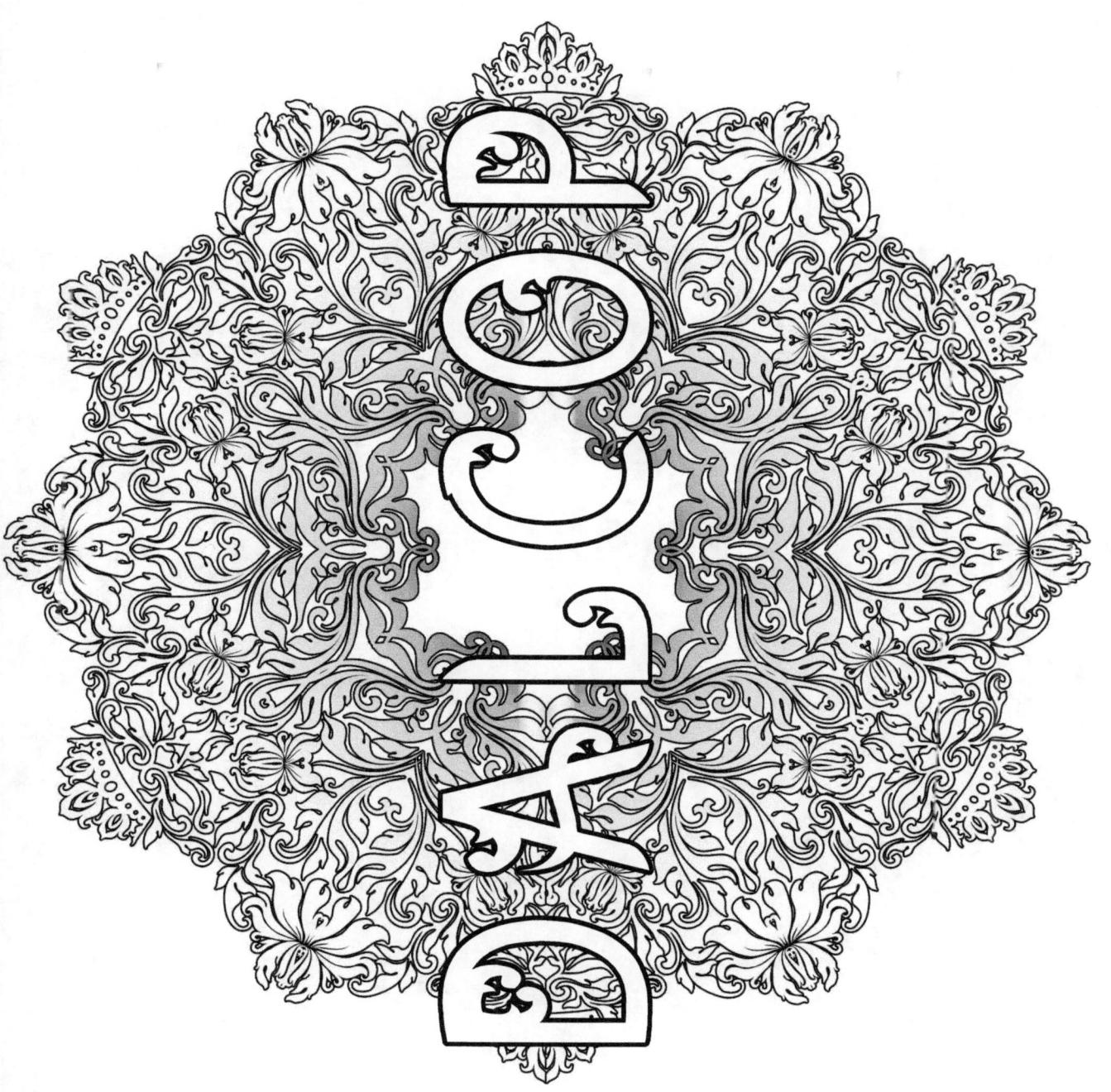

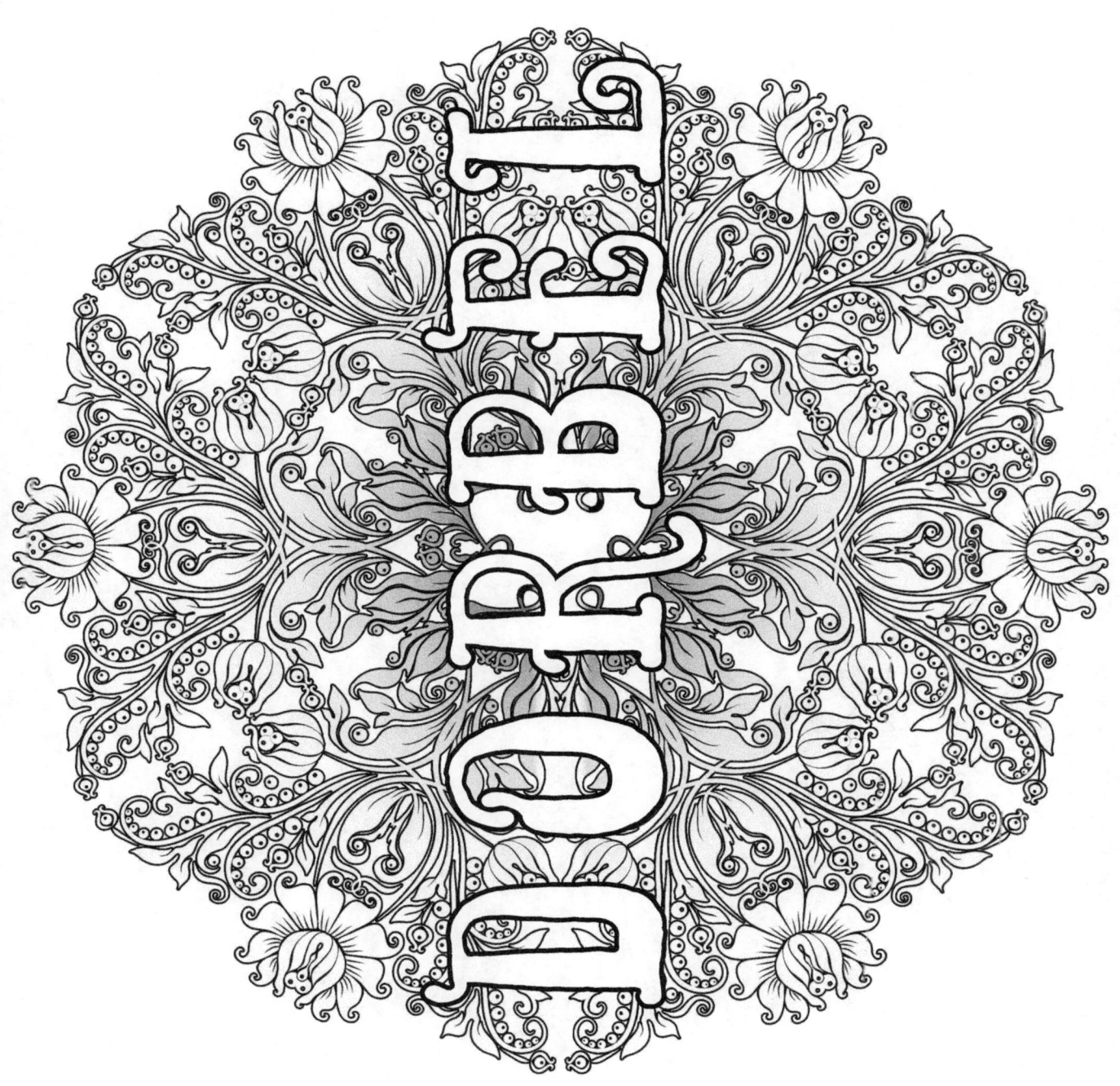

Gamahuche

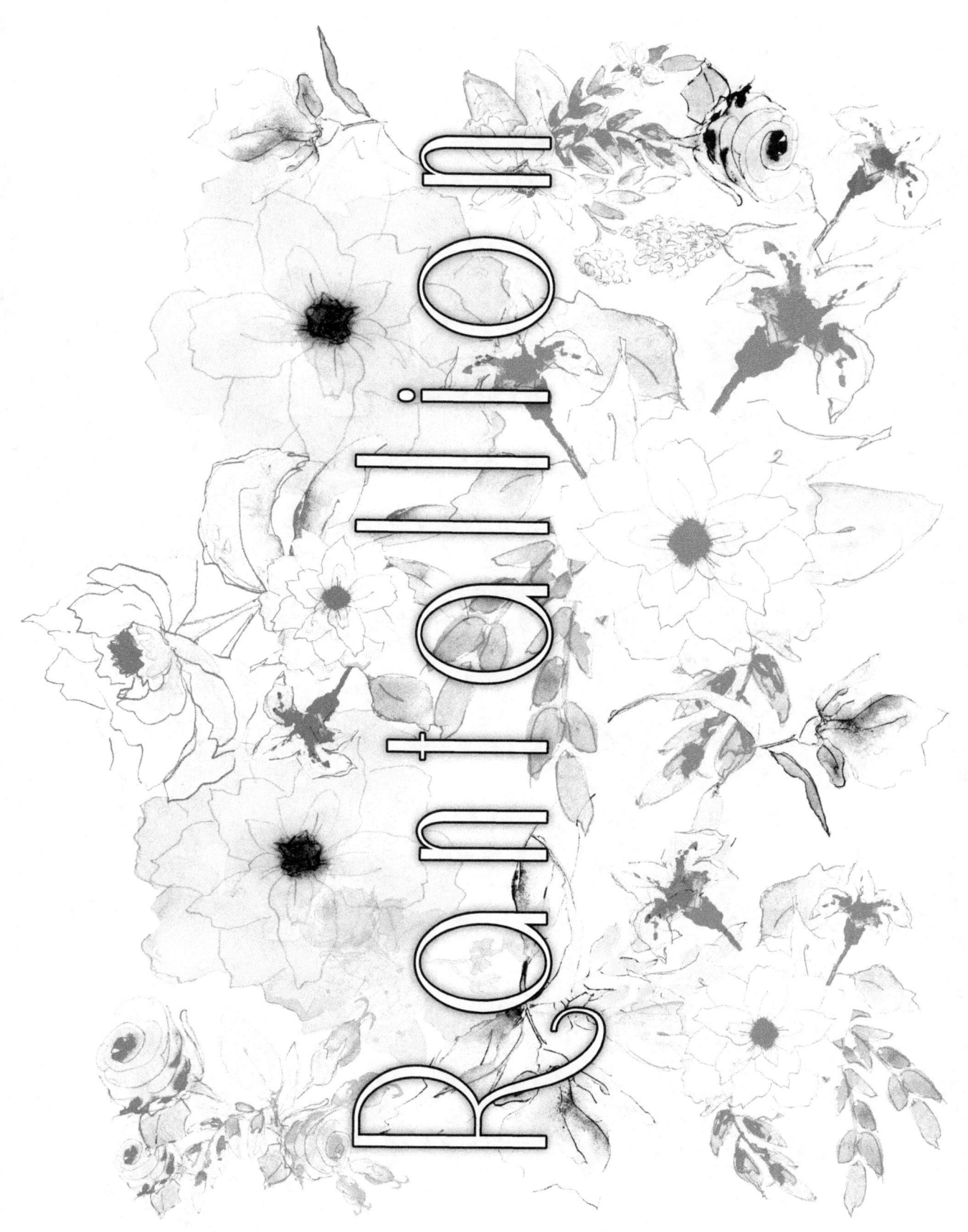

Ranunculion

Glossary / Dictionary

Amsterdam - Holland - Sterf aan kanker! (Die With Cancer)

Athens-Greece - Skata sta moutra sou (Shit In Your Face)

Bangkok - Thailand - Chuck Wow (Man Masturbate)

Barcelona - Spain - Que te den (Fuck Off)

Berlin - Germany - Fotze (Cunt)

Brussels - Belgium - Schitluis (Chickenshit)

Bucharest - Bulgaria - Cacat Cu Ochi (Piece Of Shit With Two Eyes)

Budapest - Hungary - Seggfej (Asshole)

Buenos Aires - Argentina - Culo Roto (Broken Ass)

Cairo- Egypt - Teezak Maftoh (Your Bum Is Open)

Delhi - India - Bakrichod (Goat Fucker)

Dubai - UAE - Kiss Ekh-Tak (Fuck Your Sister)

HongKong - China - Sha Bi (Douchebag)

Istanbul - Turkey - Atini Siken Kovboy (Cowboy Who Fucks His Horse)

Jakarta - Indonesia - Babi Lo (You Pig)

Johannesburg - South Africa - Draadtrekker (Wanker)

Kuala Lumpur - Malaysia - Puki Mak Kau (Your Mother's Cunt)

Los Angeles - USA - Dummy Moore (Old Actress That Can't/Won't grow up)

Las Vegas - USA - Sfacim (Semen/Jism)

London - England - Bellend (Idiot/Fool)

Macau - China - Ta Ma de - (F*ck)

Glossary / Dictionary

Madrid - Spain - Joder - (Fuck)

Mexico City - Mexico - Mamon (Cocksucker)

New York - USA - Cocksucker

Paris - France - Putain De Salope (Fucking Bitch)

Pattaya - Thailand - E Heah (Whore/Bitch)

Prague - Czech Republic - Hovno (Shit)

Rio - Brasil - Cuzão (Asshole)

Rome - Italy - Vaffanculo (Fuck You)

Sanfrancisco - USA - He Bitch

Seol - South Korea - Gae Saeki (Son Of A Bitch)

Singapore - Ho Kao Kan (Get Fucked By A Dog)

Taipei - China - Cao Ni Ma (Fuck Your Mum)

Tokyo - Japan - Kutabare (Fuck You)

Vancouver - Canada - Hoser (A Fool Doing A Fool's Work)

Vienna - Austria - Wappler (Incompetent Prick)

Bonus Section Glossary / Dictionary

Abydocomista - a liar who brags about their lies.

Beardsplitter - Victorian word for penis

Bedswerver - A British slang word for "cheater,"

Bespawler - To spit or dribble, a slobbering person, who spits when he talks.

Bobolyne - A fool

Cumberworld - Waste of space, Someone who is useless

Dalcop - Stupid

Derbel - Nincompoop

Gamahuche - Victorian word for oral sex

Rantallion - "one whose scrotum is longer than his penis."

For a bit of extra fun we have hidden the name of each city and country somewhere whithin each page. Some are easy to find, whilst others will require a keener eye... If you are unable to find all the places, drop us a line at info@rollingvoice.com and we will help you O U T .

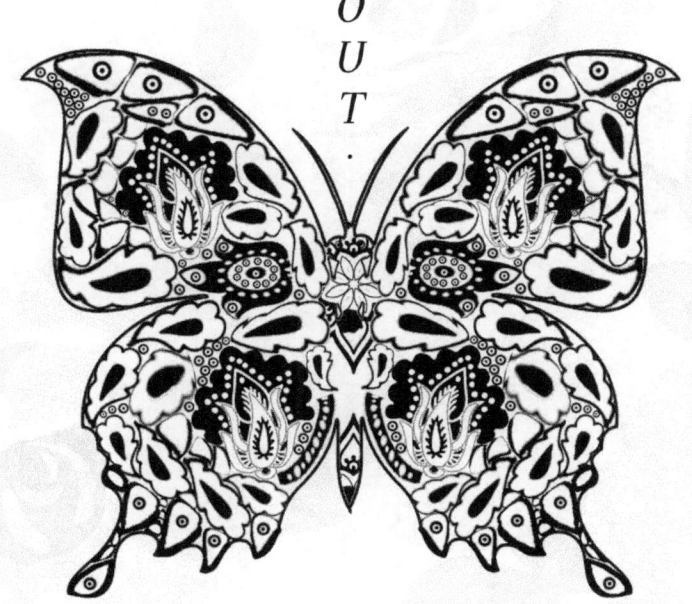

Many thanks for buying this book.
For more info please visit
www.RollingVoice.com

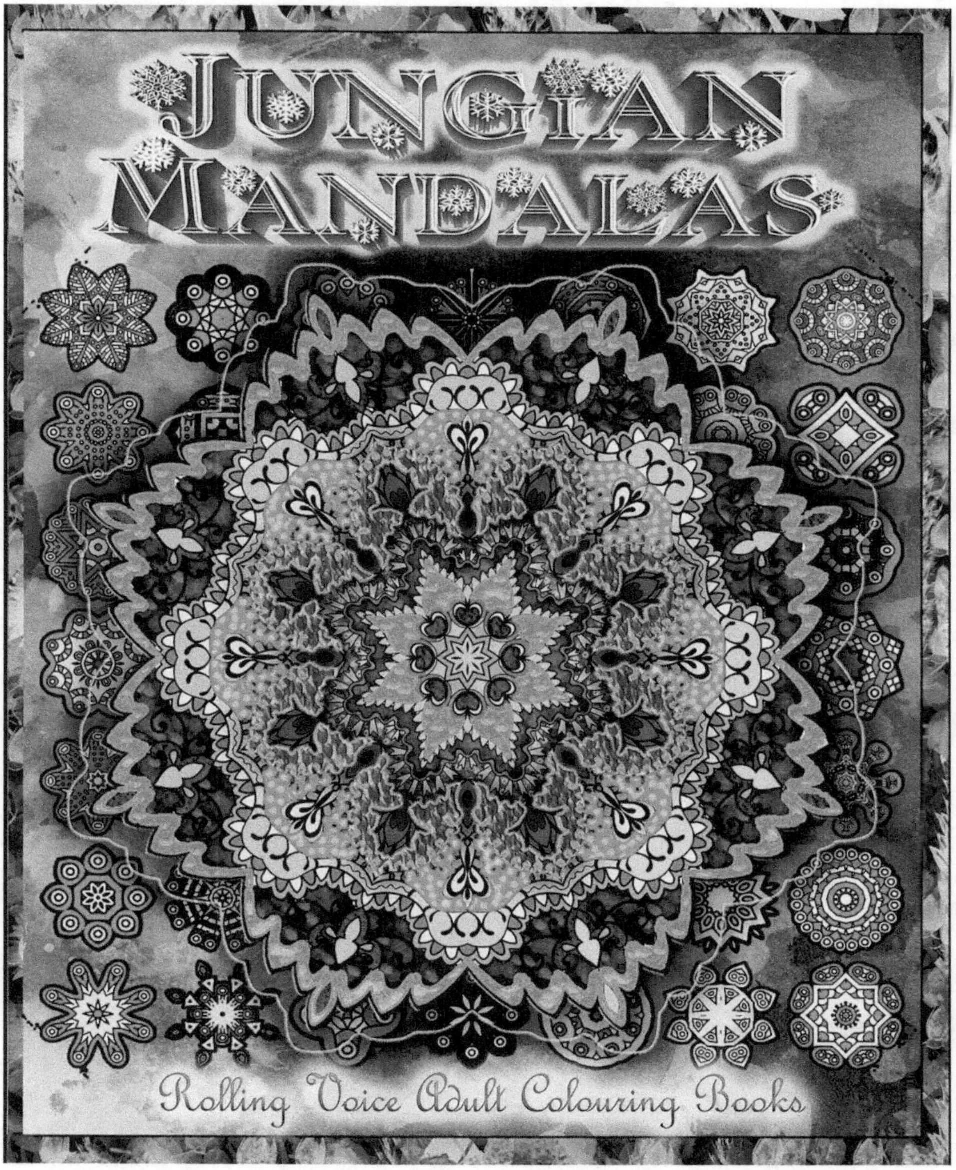

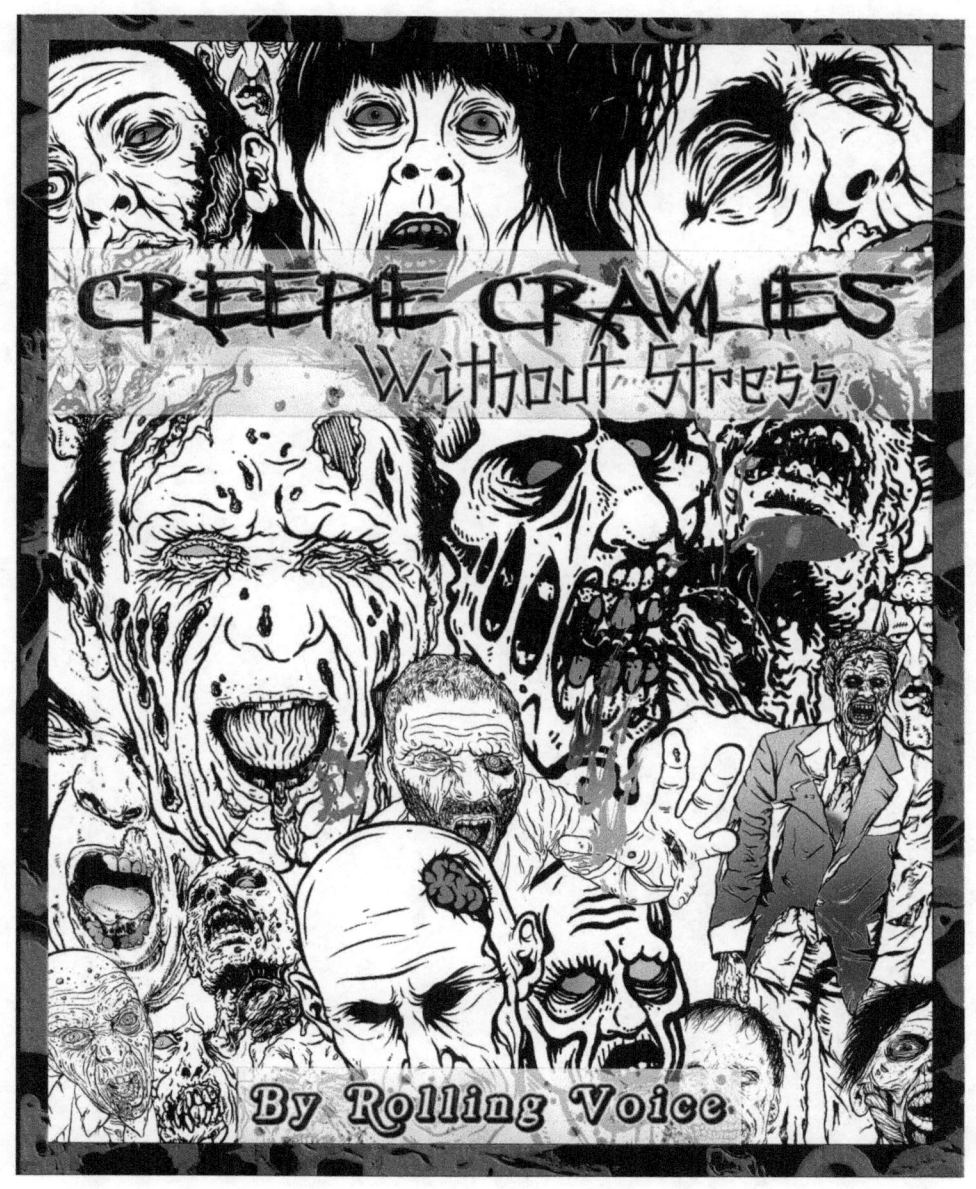

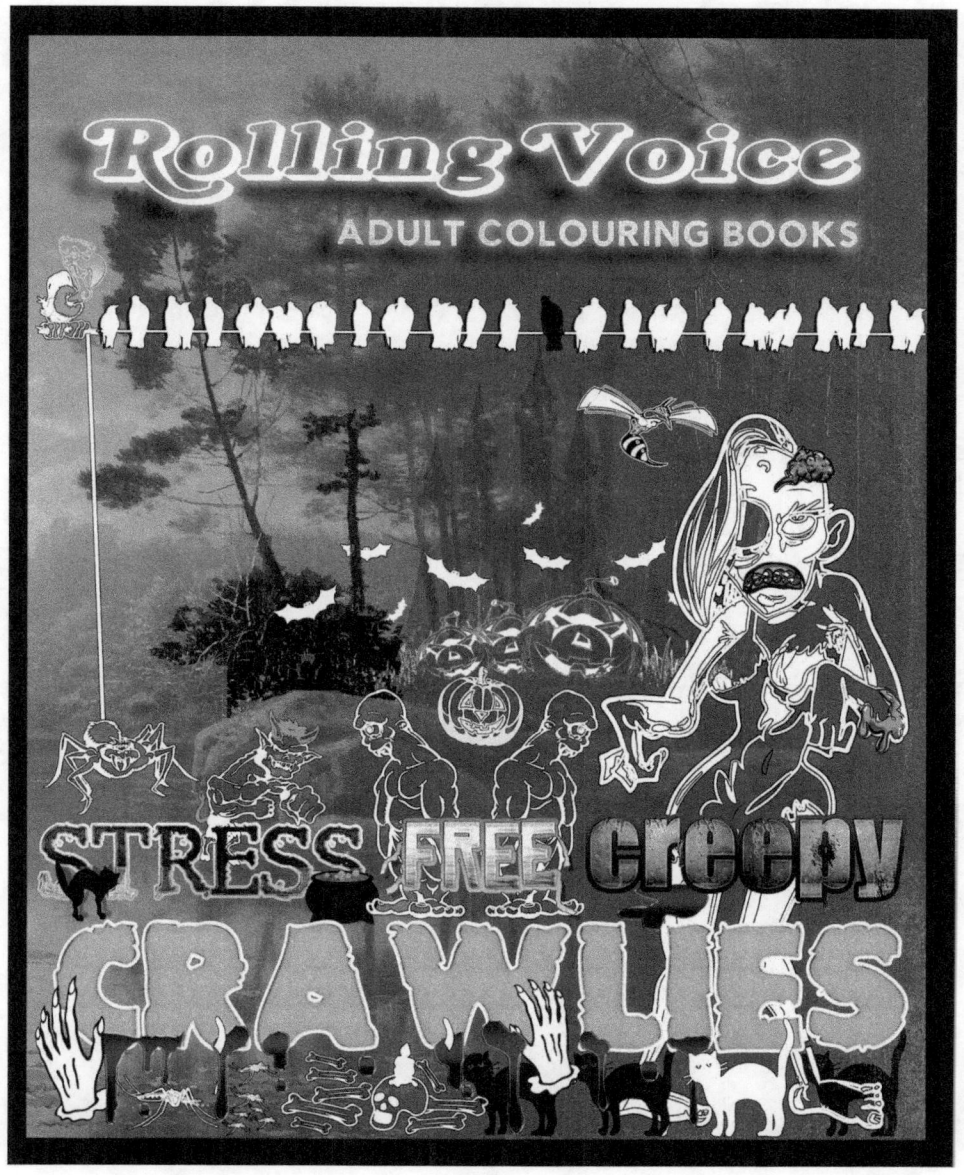

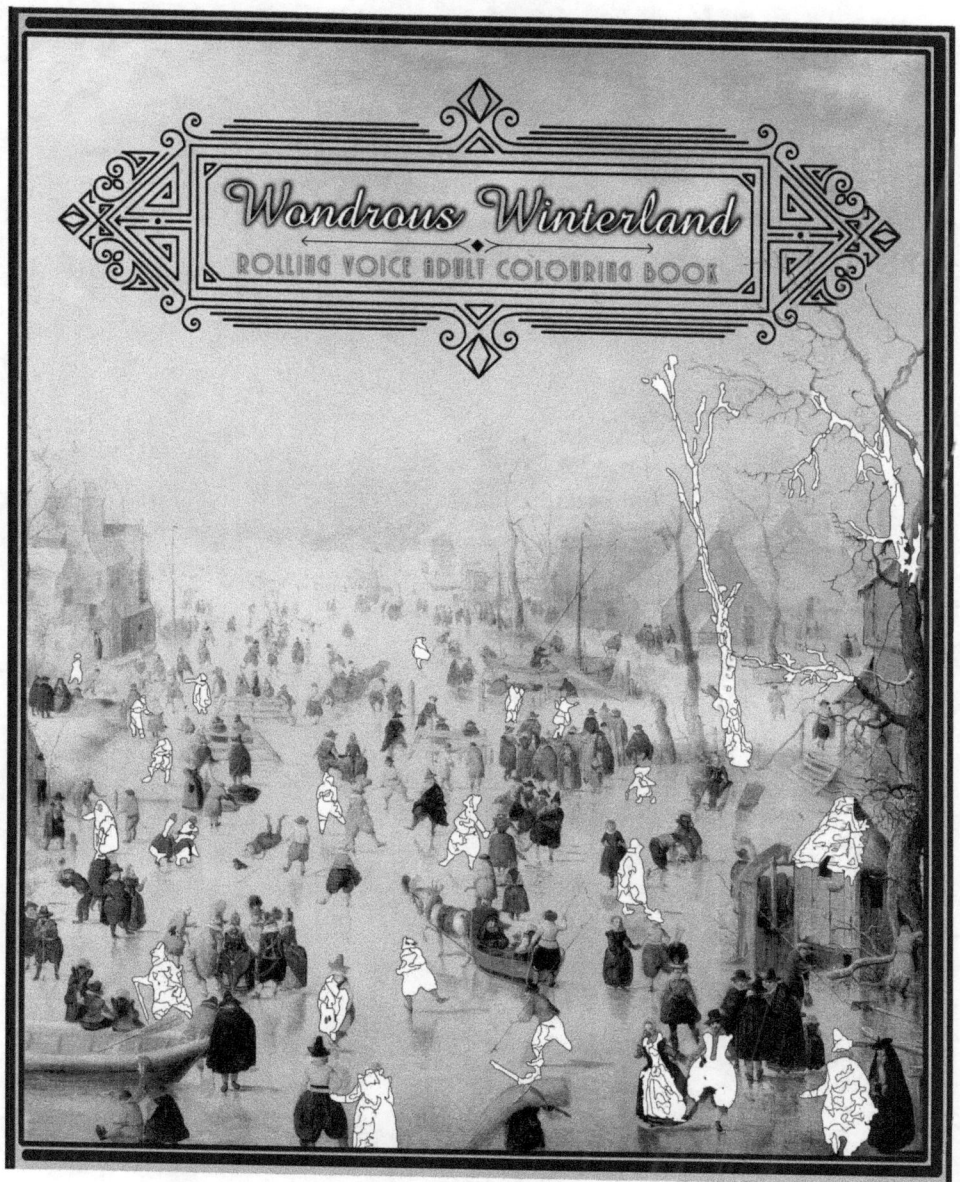

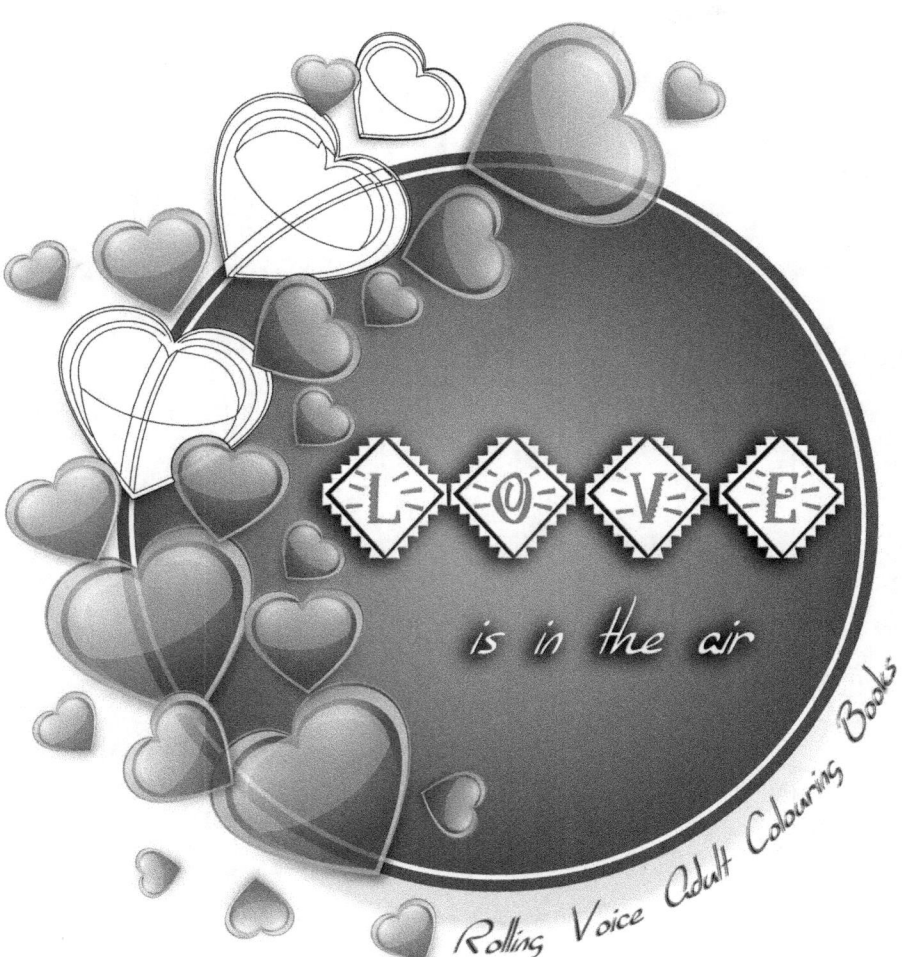